Visual Studio 2022 In-Depth

Second Edition

*Explore the Fantastic Features of
Visual Studio 2022!*

Ockert J. du Preez

www.bpbonline.com

Group Product Manager: Marianne Conor

Publishing Product Manager: Eva Brawn

Senior Editor: Connell

Content Development Editor: Melissa Monroe

Technical Editor: Anne Stokes

Copy Editor: Joe Austin

Language Support Editor: Justin Baldwin

Project Coordinator: Tyler Horan

Proofreader: Khloe Styles

Indexer: V. Krishnamurthy

Production Designer: Malcolm D'Souza

Marketing Coordinator: Kristen Kramer

First published: 2019
Second published: 2023

Published by BPB Online
WeWork, 119 Marylebone Road
London NW1 5PU

UK | UAE | INDIA | SINGAPORE

ISBN 978-93-55512-451

www.bpbonline.com

Dedicated to

Elmarie

Michaela

Winton

Björn

About the Author

- **Ockert J. du Preez** has been in the coding industry for 20+ years and has written hundreds of developer articles over the years detailing his programming quests and adventures. These can be found on CodeGuru, Developer.com and Database Journal.

He knows a broad spectrum of development languages including: C++, C#, VB.NET, JavaScript and HTML.

He has written the following books:

- Visual Studio 2019 In-Depth (BpB Publications)
- JavaScript for Gurus (BpB Publications)
- Building Cross-Platform Modern Apps using Visual Studio Code (VS Code)
- High Performance Enterprise Apps using C# 10 and .NET 6.0

He was the Technical Editor for the following books

- Professional C++, 5th Edition by Marc Gregoire
- C++ Software Interoperability for Windows Programmers by Adam Gladstone

He was a Microsoft Most Valuable Professional for .NET (2008–2017).

Acknowledgement

○ I want to thank my family for all their support, their belief in me and their never-ending support.

I wish to extend a special thank you for everyone at Cowboy Café for bringing me coffee and allowing me to write this book in their cozy atmosphere.

My gratitude also goes to the team at BPB Publications for their patience and support in writing this book.

On another personal note: I'd like to thank everyone that never believed in me and always said that I would amount to nothing, without negativity, positivity never prospers.

Preface

This book peeks into every corner of the Visual Studio IDE and help you get started with the latest 2022 version. Right from installation, you'll discover new areas within the tool, and also the optimal way to use the features you may already know. You'll learn, for example, how to extend Visual Studio with your own customizations, so that you can make it perform the way you want. You will then explore everything about .NET 6, Diagnose and debug applications and all the Collaboration tools in Visual Studio 2022.You will learn about the new AI IntelliCode, .NET MAUI and the C++ 20 features. Lastly you will explore Visual Studio 2022 on different platforms such as Linux, and macOS

The details are listed below.

Chapter 1 focuses on Installing Visual Studio 2022. It covers all the options and Add-ons to install and explore the new Visual Studio 2022 features.

Chapter 2 focuses on all the new and exciting features of .NET 6.

Chapter 3 This chapter will cover the new and enhanced features in the C# language.

Chapter 4 inspects the Visual Studio 2022 IDE and examine its features and updates from previous versions of Visual Studio.

Chapter 5 in this chapter, we will explore the new AI IntelliCode and its AI capabilities to cater for a better coding experience.

Chapter 6 discusses all the built-in tools in Visual Studio 2022. It will describe their purpose as well as explain how to use them.

Chapter 7 In this chapter you will learn about the awesome debugging tools Visual Studio 2022 has as well as their innerworkings.

Chapter 8 Because the web is a completely different platform than Desktop applications, you need special tools to help with styling and bug fixing. Chapter 8 digs into tools dedicated to the ASP.NET environment.

Chapter 9 explains the need for simulators, emulators and tools that help with creating beautiful responsive mobile apps for any market.

Chapter 10 In the world of Cloud Computing, Visual Studio 2022 provides the best tools for working with Microsoft Azure. Chapter 10 explores Azure tools and more.

Chapter 11 Visual Studio 2022 includes support for C++ 20, Chapter explores some of its new features.

APPENDIX A This covers Cross-Platform applications in Visual Studio 2022 as well as Visual Studio for Mac features.

Code Bundle and Coloured Images

Please follow the link to download the
Code Bundle and the *Coloured Images* of the book:

https://rebrand.ly/8b48fd

The code bundle for the book is also hosted on GitHub at **https://github.com/bpbpublications/Visual-Studio-2022-In-Depth-2nd-Edition**. In case there's an update to the code, it will be updated on the existing GitHub repository.

We have code bundles from our rich catalogue of books and videos available at **https://github.com/bpbpublications**. Check them out!

Errata

We take immense pride in our work at BPB Publications and follow best practices to ensure the accuracy of our content to provide with an indulging reading experience to our subscribers. Our readers are our mirrors, and we use their inputs to reflect and improve upon human errors, if any, that may have occurred during the publishing processes involved. To let us maintain the quality and help us reach out to any readers who might be having difficulties due to any unforeseen errors, please write to us at :

errata@bpbonline.com

Your support, suggestions and feedbacks are highly appreciated by the BPB Publications' Family.

Piracy

If you come across any illegal copies of our works in any form on the internet, we would be grateful if you would provide us with the location address or website name. Please contact us at **business@bpbonline.com** with a link to the material.

If you are interested in becoming an author

If there is a topic that you have expertise in, and you are interested in either writing or contributing to a book, please visit **www.bpbonline.com**. We have worked with thousands of developers and tech professionals, just like you, to help them share their insights with the global tech community. You can make a general application, apply for a specific hot topic that we are recruiting an author for, or submit your own idea.

Reviews

Please leave a review. Once you have read and used this book, why not leave a review on the site that you purchased it from? Potential readers can then see and use your unbiased opinion to make purchase decisions. We at BPB can understand what you think about our products, and our authors can see your feedback on their book. Thank you!

For more information about BPB, please visit **www.bpbonline.com**.

Table of Contents

Section - I
Getting to Know the
Visual Studio 2022 IDE

Introduction

In the Getting Started section, we will discover all the installation options as well as learn how to install Visual Studio 2022 to suit our needs. We will have a look at the **Integrated Development Environment (IDE)** and all its associated windows. In *Chapter 2, Having a look at .NET 6, we* will learn about the new features of .NET 6, it's history and the .NET 6 enhancements. Next, in *Chapter 3, C# 9 Language & Coding Changes*, we will have a look at Intellisense and how it can save us hundreds of keystrokes while writing a big program. Finally, we look at the language changes in C# 9.0 and .NET Core 3.0.

This section will have the following chapters:

- **Chapter 1** – Getting Started with Visual Studio
- **Chapter 2** – Having a look at .NET 6
- **Chapter 3** - C# 9 Language & Coding Changes
- **Chapter 4** – Digging in the Visual Studio 2022

CHAPTER 1
Getting Started with Visual Studio 2022

The first version of Visual Studio was released in 1997, and it was the first time all Microsoft's programming tools were integrated into one common IDE. Now, more than 20 years later, the technology landscape has changed tremendously, and Visual Studio has adapted continuously with it. Therefore, Visual Studio 2022 includes the best and newest tools to work with modern-day problems and technologies.

This chapter focuses on Installing Visual Studio 2022. It covers all the options and Add-ons to install and explore the new Visual Studio 2022 features including DevOps, IntelliCode, new Debugging windows updates, new Open Windows and many more!

Structure

In this chapter, we will cover the following topics:

- Why Visual Studio 2022?
- New features of Visual Studio
- Requirements and prerequisites
- Visual Studio 2022 editions

- Installation options

- Choose what to install

- Launching Visual Studio 2022

Objectives

After reading this chapter the reader will understand how to install Visual Studio 2022. We will explore the various windows inside Visual Studio 2022. We will also look at the history of Visual Studio and explore some of its great features.

Why Visual Studio 2022?

The answer is simple: Productivity. Visual Studio 2022 allows us to create, debug and deploy Desktop, Web and Mobile applications with great ease. Visual Studio 2022 boasts a powerful debugger and vast amount of debugging windows which aid in exception handling and debugging. Developer productivity in Visual Studio 2022 has increased immensely with the widening of the Code Editor, Code Health and Document Indicator tools and quick project creation. Working in a team is also easier and better with the addition of DevOps. Visual Studio 2022 has an inviting IDE with windows such as Solution Explorer, Server Explorer, Team Explorer, Data Sources, Properties Window and the Toolbox Window.

Visual Studio 2022 also has a ton of new features which we will delve into further. First, let us understand some of the well-known Windows for the newbies reading this book.

The Solution Explorer

The Solution Explorer Window shows all the files in our projects including classes, references, forms or pictures. It serves as a quick way to switch between windows, as well as do project or solution-oriented tasks as follows:

- Renaming files

- Adding references quickly

- Removing project items

- Adding project items

Figure 1.1: Solution Explorer

The Properties window

The Properties window hosts all the properties of an object like: Forms, any controls on the Form, Web Pages, the Project or Solution itself. Properties are characteristics of objects, for example its name, size, location, colour or file name. Properties describe objects. Please take a look at the following screenshot:

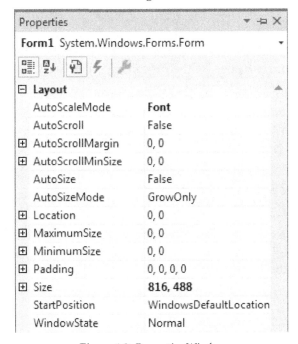

Figure 1.2: Properties Window

Inside the Properties window we can also add the event handlers for the controls on the Form or web page, or mobile screen. Please take a look at the following screenshot:

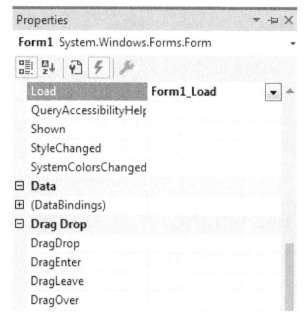

Figure 1.3: Properties Window Events

Each object has different events, and our job as developers would be to program these events to suit our purpose. In the preceding image we will notice that **Load** has an event. This event is named **Form1_Load**.

The naming convention of an event is: **ObjectName_EventName**. The specific event's name gets added to the Object's name. This makes it easy for us to identify and search for certain events when the need arises.

Data Sources window

The Data Sources window allows us to add data sources to our project. A Data Source is explained as a place or object from which we obtain data. This can be a database such as Microsoft SQL Server, Microsoft Access, Oracle, and so on. The tab for this window might not always be visible. Find it by clicking **View**, **Other Windows**, **Data Sources**.

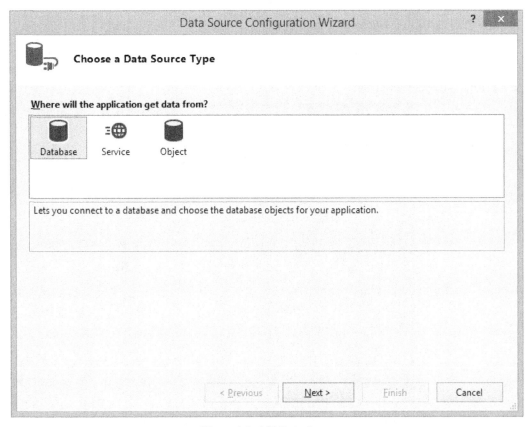

Figure 1.4: *Add Data Source*

Specify the location of the obtained data. On the next screen specify the table name, Stored Procedure name or query name which will fetch the data or contains the data. After a Data Source is added we can use it throughout our Windows form, web page or mobile screen.

Server Explorer window

The Server Explorer window shows the details of all the servers that we are connected to. These include Cloud Services, Databases and Virtual Machines. Please take a look at the following screenshot:

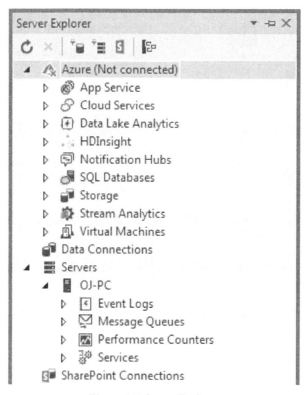

Figure 1.5: *Server Explorer*

It is broken up into four parts as follows:

- Azure which includes:
    - o App Services
    - o Cloud Services
    - o Data Lake Analytics
    - o SQL Databases
    - o Storage
    - o Virtual Machines
- Data Connections

- Servers which includes:
    - o   Event Logs
    - o   Services
    - o   Performance Counters
    - o   Message Queues
- SharePoint Connections

Azure

Microsoft Azure is a cloud computing service operated by Microsoft to manage applications through the use of Microsoft-managed data centers. Azure provides **software as a service (SaaS)**, **platform as a service (PaaS)** and **infrastructure as a service (IaaS)** and also supports many tools and different programming languages and frameworks which we will quickly discuss.

App Services

Azure App Service is a managed **Platform as a Service (PaaS)** that integrates Mobile Services, Microsoft Azure Websites, and BizTalk Services into one single service. This adds new capabilities that enable integration with on-premises or cloud systems.

Azure Cloud Services

Azure Cloud Services, also a PaaS, is designed to support applications that are scalable, reliable, and most importantly, inexpensive to operate. Azure Cloud Services are hosted on **Virtual Machines (VMs)**. You can install your own software on them, and access them remotely.

Data Lake Analytics

Azure Data Lake Analytics is an analytics job service that simplifies big data. You don't have to deploy or configure hardware, you simply write queries to transform your data and extract insights.

SQL Databases

SQL Azure is Microsoft's cloud database service. With SQL Azure organizations can store relational data in the cloud and scale the size of their databases depending on the business needs.

Storage

Azure Storage is a service providing cloud storage that is highly available, secure, durable, and scalable. It includes Azure Blobs, Azure Data Lake Storage Gen2, Azure Files, Azure Queues, and Azure Tables.

Virtual Machines

Azure Windows Virtual Machines provides secure, high-scale, on-demand, virtualized infrastructure using Windows Server.

Data connections

As explained in the Data Source window section, data connections can also be added here. After a connection has been made, a Data Source gets created and added in the Server Explorer window as well as the Data Sources window.

Servers

The Servers in the Services window are the actual servers you are connected to. The items such as the Event Log and Services help testing services you create and deploy to these servers. It saves a lot of time. Message queue allows us to trace various application messages that gets sent to the servers. Performance Counters shows how the applications perform and is quick to detect the problem.

SharePoint connections

SharePoint is a web-based collaborative platform. In Server Explorer we can navigate through all the components of a SharePoint site on our system.

Toolbox

The Toolbox contains all the controls, or tools, that we can add to our form, web page or mobile screen. Windows forms controls differ from ASP.NET Web Forms Controls that further differ from mobile or cloud controls.

For example: A Windows textbox behaves differently on a web application and a mobile application. On a mobile platform a Windows textbox is known as an **entry field**. In all three platforms similar controls are used differently and programmed differently.

ASP.NET includes controls such as DropDown List, Hidden Fields and Ad Rotators, whereas a Windows Forms project includes a ComboBox (which is similar to the ASP.NET's DropDown List), Panel. A mobile application includes different controls specific to the mobile platform, which will not work on a Windows forms application.

In the following figure we will see the Windows forms toolbox as well as an ASP. NET web form toolbox. Please take a look at the following screenshot:

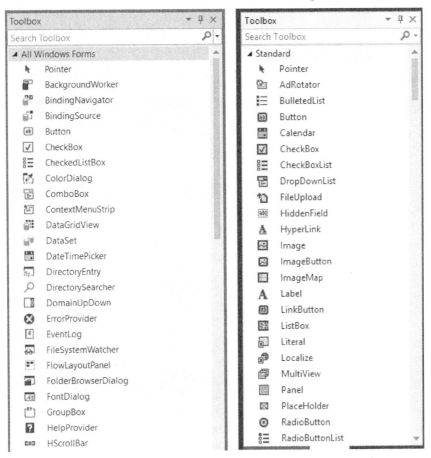

Figure 1.6: *Examples of the different Toolboxes*

New features of Visual Studio 2022

Visual Studio 2022 has a lot of new and exciting features and changes, including the following:

New project dialog box

The new project dialog box, *Figure 1.7*, features an improved search experience and filters to create projects faster:

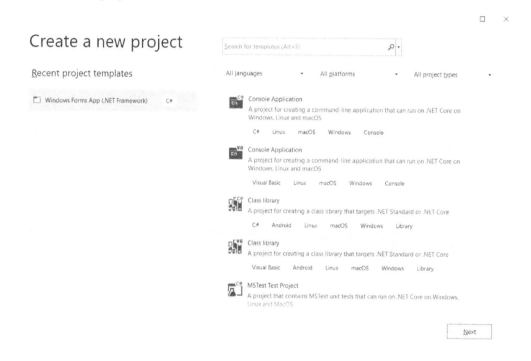

Figure 1.7: *New Project dialog box*

IntelliCode completions

Notice on the left side of following *figure 1.8*, there's a small purple icon. This is for setting up IntelliCode completions. IntelliCode predicts the next piece of code based on the code's current context, and presents it as an inline suggestion to the right of the cursor.

Document indicator

Document indicator enables us to check and maintain our code's issues:

Figure 1.8: *Document Health Indicator*

Solution filter

Solution filter files enables us to choose which projects should be loaded when a solution is opened. To save a solution as a filter, please right click on an existing solution and select **Save As Solution Filter**. This is shown in the following figure:

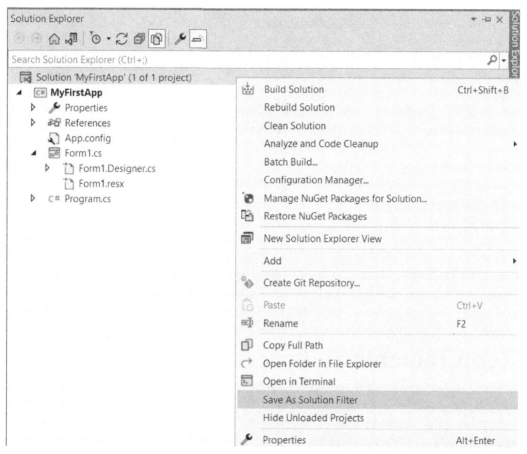

Figure 1.9: Solution Filter

Visual Studio 2022 updates

You can decide how and when to install Visual Studio 2022 updates. When we click **Tools**, **Options** we will see the **Product Updates** field, as shown in the following figure:

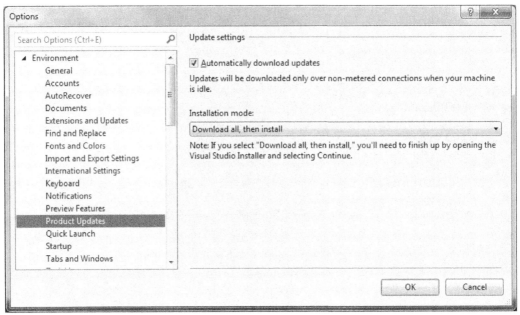

Figure 1.10: Updates

Requirements and prerequisites

In order to install or run Visual Studio 2022, the following minimum requirements must be met.

Supported Operating Systems

64-bit is recommended for the following Operating Systems:

- Windows 10 (Home, Professional, Education, and Enterprise) version 1703 or higher

- Windows Server 2016 (Standard and Datacenter)

- Windows 8.1 (Core, Professional, and Enterprise) with Update 2919355

- Windows Server 2012 R2 (Essentials, Standard, Datacenter) with Update 2919355

- Windows 7 SP1 (Home Premium, Professional, Enterprise, Ultimate) with latest Windows Updates

Hardware

We need the following hardware requirements:

- 1.8 GHz or faster processor. Quad-core or better is recommended for Windows.

- 4 GB of RAM.

- Minimum of 850MB up to 210 GB of available space on a hard disk, depending on the selected features installed. Installations typically require 20-50 GB of free space.

- A Video card that supports a minimum display resolution of 720p (1280 by 720); Visual Studio will work best at a resolution of WXGA (1366 by 768) or higher.

Supported languages

Visual Studio is available in fourteen different languages such as:

- English

- Chinese (Simplified)

- Chinese (Traditional)

- Czech

- French

- German

- Italian

- Japanese

- Korean

- Polish

- Portuguese (Brazil)

- Russian

- Spanish

- Turkish

Select the language we want for Visual Studio at the time of installation and Visual Studio Installer itself becomes available in the language we selected.

Visual Studio 2022 Editions

Visual Studio 2022 comes in various editions as follows:

Visual Studio 2022 Community

The Community Edition of Visual Studio 2022 is free. However, it does not have all the features that the Professional and Enterprise Editions have. Visual Studio Community 2022 is a fully-featured **Integrated Development Environment (IDE)** that can be used for creating applications for Android, iOS, Windows, plus web applications and cloud services.

Visual Studio 2022 Professional

Visual Studio 2022 Professional includes professional developer tools and services for individuals or small teams. The professional edition includes everything a professional developer needs to build desktop applications, Web applications as well as mobile applications.

Visual Studio 2022 Enterprise

Visual Studio 2022 Enterprise is an integrated solution for teams of any size with demanding scale and quality needs. It includes all the features Visual Studio has to offer. We can take advantage of all the debugging and testing tools included such as: *Coded UI Testing, Xamarin Inspector, Code Coverage,* and *Live Unit Testing.*

Installation options

Visual Studio 2022 provides a lot of options to install. It all depends on our space, time, and requirements. The more we select, the longer the installation will run. Installation time has been reduced drastically since Visual Studio 2017, and Visual Studio 2022 is even faster.

We can select from the following options to install:

Windows

The following options are available for installing Visual Studio 2022 on Windows:

- **.NET desktop development**: We can create **Windows Presentation Foundation (WPF)** applications and Window Forms applications. Windows Presentation Foundation is a graphical system by Microsoft for displaying user interfaces in Windows applications. Windows Forms allow us to create powerful Windows-based applications.

- **Desktop development with C++**: We can create applications using Win32 APIs and the Windows SDK in C++.

- **Universal Windows Platform development**: With Windows 10 came the Universal Windows Platform. This is a common application platform that can run Windows 10. These include **Internet of Things** (**IoT**), mobile, *Xbox, HoloLens, Surface Hub* and PC's and laptops.

Web and Cloud

The following options are available for installing Visual Studio 2022 for Web and Cloud:

- **ASP.NET and web development**: We create web applications with ASP.NET. We design the pages through either the design view, or HTML, CSS and JavaScript code. Then, we add C# code at the back-end for business logic or data access.

- **Azure development**: Azure allows us to build, debug, deploy and manage scalable multi-platform apps and services easily.

- **Python development**: Python is a programming language best suited for working in data analytics, test automation, and machine learning. Visual Studio 2022 enables us to program in Python and includes the necessary Python tools.

- **Node.js development**: Node.js is a JavaScript framework created for server side scripting specifically. Visual Studio includes tools that aid in creating decent .Node.js projects.

- **Data storage and processing**: The data storage and processing workload provides us the tools to develop queries against databases, data warehouses and on-premises or Azure data lakes. It supports SQL, **Unified SQL** (**U-SQL**), and Hive.

- **Data science and analytical applications**: The data science and analytical applications workload joins the strengths of R, Python and F#, with their respective runtime distributions.

- **Office/SharePoint development**: The Office/SharePoint development workload provides all the tools we need in order to extend Office and SharePoint.

Mobile and gaming

The following options are available for installing Visual Studio 2022 for mobile and gaming:

- **Mobile development with .NET**: We can build native iOS, Android, and **Universal Windows Platform (UWP)** apps using C# and Xamarin.

- **Game development with Unity**: We can create 2D and 3D games and interactive content with the Unity engine.

- **Mobile development with C++**: We can create and build native C++ apps for Android and iOS.

- **Game development with C++**: We can create games that run on Windows, Xbox.

Other toolsets

The following options are available for installing Visual Studio 2022 for Extension development, or Linux development:

- **Visual Studio extension development**: Create extensions for Visual Studio using any of Visual Basic, C++, C#.

- **Linux development with C++**: Write C++ code for Linux servers, desktops and devices.

- **.NET Core cross-platform development**: .NET Core is an open-source, general-purpose development platform. It supports Windows, macOS, and Linux and can be used to build cloud, device, and IoT applications.

Choosing what to install

Currently we can download the Community Edition Preview of Visual Studio by going to the following link in our browser:

https://visualstudio.microsoft.com/thank-you-downloading-visual-studio/?sku=community&ch=pre&rel=17

> **Note: Link may change after the time of writing**

1. Once we have downloaded it, double click on the setup file. We will then be presented with the following screen:

Figure 1.11: *Start Visual Studio 2022 Installation*

2. Click **Continue**.

3. *Figure 1.12* displays the screen informing us that the installer is fetching and installing the necessary setup files:

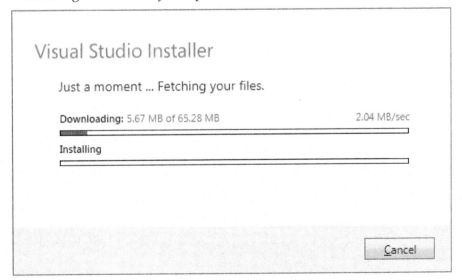

Figure 1.12: *Installing Files*

4. *Figure 1.13* displays the screen once all the files have been fetched and almost installed:

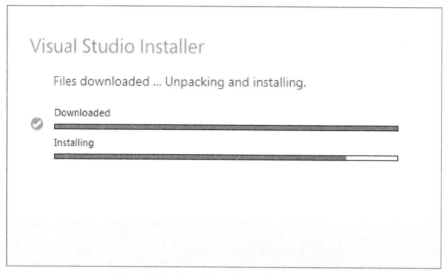

Figure 1.13: *Setup Files almost done installing*

5. After the setup files have been installed, the Visual Studio Installer will then display all the options as explained in the previous section.

6. The following *figures 1.14* to *1.16* displays all these options. *Figure 1.14* displays all the Windows Workloads available:

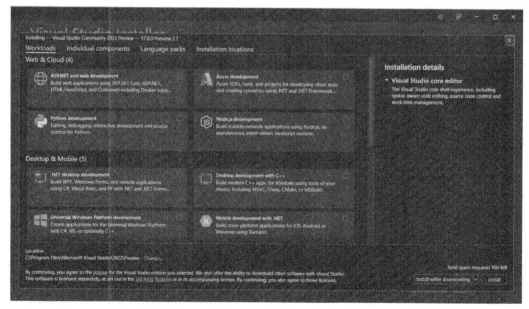

Figure 1.14: *Windows*

7. The following figure illustrates the Web and Cloud Workloads that include ASP.NET and Web Development, Python development, and Node.js development.

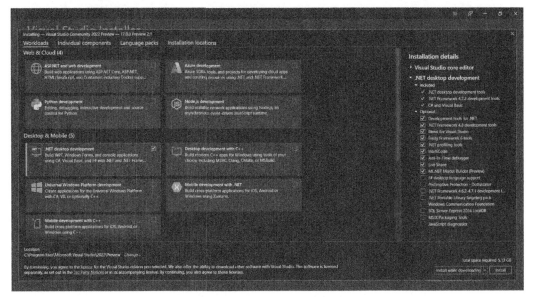

Figure 1.15: *Web & Cloud Workloads*

Mobile and gaming Workloads allows you to install options such as Unity (which is a very good platform for authoring good games) and .NET.

When you want to create extensions for Visual Studio or author code for Linux, the other Toolsets Workload is for you.

We can choose to install the options while downloading, or download everything first, then install, as shown in *Figure 1.16*.

8. After we have made our selections on what to install, click on **Install**. A screen similar to the following figure will appear:

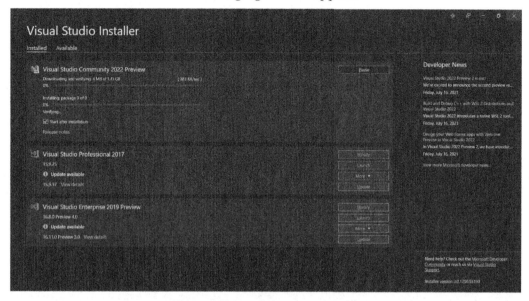

Figure 1.16: Install Visual Studio 2022

We can pause the installation any time but ensure that we have a decent internet connection with enough data to download all the features.

Launching Visual Studio 2022

When launching Visual Studio 2022 for the first time, it will prompt us that the application is busy setting up our environment based on our choices and its necessary settings.

Figures 1.17 and *1.18* displays the new Visual Studio 2022 start screen. Here, it is so much easier and quicker to get started on our current projects, as they are all displayed neatly. Starting a new project from scratch is also easier with the new template window allowing us to search and find our favourite templates quickly. Please take a look at the following screenshot:

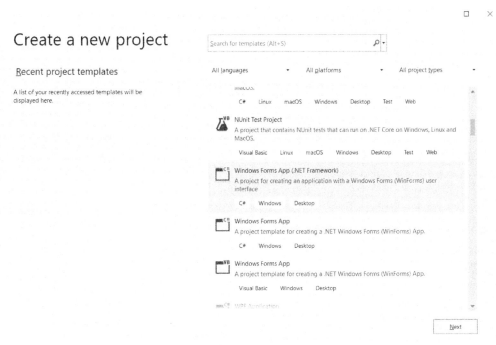

Figure 1.17: Open Recent Project

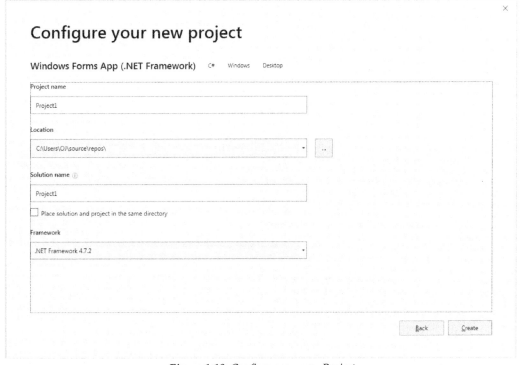

Figure 1.18: Configure our new Project

A new project will be created according to our specifications.

Conclusion

In this chapter we were introduced to Visual Studio 2022. We learned about the different Editions of Visual Studio 2022 – Preview, Community, Professional and Enterprise, and their differences. We learned what the requirements are to install Visual Studio 2022, and then we learned how to install Visual Studio 2022 and what options are available to suit our needs. We have learned about some new features such as the New Project and Open Project dialog boxes and the debugging windows and how the new features can increase productivity. We explored the Visual Studio 2022 IDE and learned about some of the important windows such as the Server Explorer, Toolbox and Properties window.

In the next chapter, *Having a look at .NET 6*, we will learn about the new features of .NET 6, it's history and the .NET 6 enhancements.

Key topics

- Server Explorer

- Properties Window

- Solution Explorer

- Visual Studio 2022 Editions

Points to remember

- Visual Studio 2022 Professional includes professional developer tools and services for individuals or small teams.

- The properties window hosts all the properties of an object like: Forms, any controls on the form, web pages, the project, or solution itself.

- Visual Studio 2022 boasts a powerful debugger and vast amount of debugging windows which aid in exception handling and debugging. Developer productivity in Visual Studio 2022 has increased immensely with the widening of the Code Editor, Code Health and Document Indicator tools and quick project creation. Working in a team is also easier and better with the addition of DevOps. Visual Studio 2022 also has an inviting IDE with windows such as the Solution Explorer, Server Explorer, Team Explorer, Data Sources, Properties Window, and the Toolbox Window.

Questions

1. What is the function of the Solution Filter?

2. What does IntelliCode do?

3. What is the function of the Toolbox?

Answers

1. Solution Filter Files enables us to choose which projects should be loaded when a Solution is opened.

2. IntelliCode predicts the next piece of code based on the code's current context, and presents it as an inline suggestion to the right of the cursor.

3. The Toolbox contains all the controls, or Tools, that we can add to our Form, Web Page or Mobile screen.

CHAPTER 2
Having a Look at .NET 6

Introduction

.NET has come a very long way since its first release over two decades ago. It changed the world of programming forever by providing a better way to do things.

Where older development technologies found it difficult to communicate with each other, .NET made it easier. .NET has also been able to move forward with the technology trends, thus making development easier.

Most importantly, .NET is completely object-orientated thus bridging the gap between object orientated languages and non-object-oriented languages.

Structure

In this chapter we will cover the following topics:

- .NET Framework history
- New Features in .NET 6
- .NET 6 Enhancements

Objectives

The objective of this chapter is to see how far .NET has come and discusses the new features of .NET 6. This chapter starts with the history of .NET, then provides details on the .NET framework itself. We tackle the new features and enhancements of .NET 6.

After reading this chapter, the reader will understand what the .NET Framework is, how it came about and the history of .NET. The reader will also get an insight into the new and exciting features of .NET Framework 6.

.NET Framework history

In order to understand where .NET comes from and how it originated, we first need to have a look at **Next Generation Windows Services** (**NGWS**). .Net Framework, originally named **Next Generation Windows Services** (**NGWS**), is a simplified application development. Some objectives of the first .NET Framework included:

- Providing a consistent object-oriented programming environment in the following events:
    - If the object code is stored and executed locally.
    - If the object code is executed locally but Internet-distributed.
    - If the object code is executed remotely.
- Providing a code-execution environment that:
    - Would minimize deployment as well as versioning conflicts.
    - Guarantees safe execution of code whether it is unknown third party code or semi-trusted third party code.
    - Eliminates the performance problems of scripted or interpreted environments.
- Making developer's experience consistent across varying types of applications.
- Ensuring .NET Framework code can integrate with any other code.

Components of .NET Framework

The .NET Framework consists of these two components:

- The **Common Language Runtime** (**CLR**)
- The .NET Framework class library

Let's have a look at each.

The Common Language Runtime

The **Common Language Runtime** (**CLR**) acts as a virtual agent that manages code at execution time. This provides core services such as memory management, thread management, and remoting. The runtime also enforces strict safety and code accuracy that ensures security and robustness. Code management is a fundamental principle of the runtime. Code that targets the runtime is known as managed code, while code that does not target the runtime is known as unmanaged code. Please refer to the *References* section at the end of this chapter for more information on unmanaged and managed code.

Features and benefits of the Common Language Runtime

These include:

- Managing memory, thread execution, code execution, code safety, and compilation, among other system services.

- Enforcing code access security. This means that users can trust an executable (.EXE file) embedded (for example) in a Web page that can function as it needs to, but the file cannot access their personal data, file system, or network.

- Enforcing code robustness by implementing a strict type-and-code-verification infrastructure called the **Common Type System** (**CTS**).

- Eliminating common software issues such as handling object layout, managing references to objects, releasing references these objects when they are no longer being used.

- Accelerating developer productivity.

- It is designed for the software of the future as well as software of today and yesterday.

- It is designed to enhance performance.

The .NET Framework class library (FCL)

These .NET APIs include classes, interfaces, delegates, and value types. The .NET Framework Class Library facilitates interoperability between languages whose compiler conforms to the **common language specification** (**CLS**).

The .NET Framework Class Library include classes types that perform the following functions:

- Representing base data types and exceptions.

- Encapsulating data structures.

- Performing I/O (Input / Output).

- Accessing information about loaded types.

- Invoking .NET security checks.

- The .NET Framework Class Library exposes a set of APIs and types for common functionality.

If you are not familiar with .NET in general, the next topics might be a tad confusing. The next few topics explore the world of .Net 6 and its improvements and new features.

New features in .NET 6

As with the previous iterations of the .NET Framework, .NET 6 includes a tonne of new features. These include:

Blazor desktop apps

Blazor is a framework on which we can build interactive client-side web **user interfaces (UI)**. With .Net 6, it has been extended to enable developers to write Blazor desktop apps empowering developers to create hybrid client apps that combines web and native UI in a native client application.

Blazor desktop is built on top of .NET Multi-platform App UI (as discussed later in this chapter) and is targeted at web developers wanting to provide rich client and offline experiences for users.

Blazor desktop includes a WebView control that can render content from an embedded Blazor web server that serves either Blazor or web content such as JavaScript and CSS, for example. This means that Blazor desktop can be used for Blazor and web technologies that caters to all aspects of the client application experience, or for targeted functionality within a native app.

.NET SDK Optional Workload improvements

Software Development Kit (SDK) workloads enables us to add support for new application types such as mobile and WebAssembly without increasing the size of the SDK.

This feature includes list and update verbs, providing a sense of the expected final experience. We can quickly establish our preferred environment and keep it up-to-date over time.

To find out which workloads have been installed, use the following command in the Visual Studio 2022 Developer Command Prompt: dotnet workload list. All the dotnet workload commands operate in the context of the given SDK.

To update all installed workloads to the newest version, use the following command in the Visual Studio 2022 Developer Command Prompt: dotnet workload update. Here, update queries nuget.org or updated workload manifests updates local manifests, downloads new versions of the installed workloads, and then removes all the old versions of a workload.

To install a workload use the following command in the Visual Studio 2022 Developer Command Prompt: dotnet workload install [bundle], where bundle can be `microsoft-net-sdk-blazorwebassembly-aot` for Blazor or dotnet workload install `microsoft-ios-sdk-full`, for example.

To see this in action, follow these steps:

1. Press the Windows key on the keyboard.

2. Search for Developer. Windows should bring up a list similar to *Figure 2.1*.

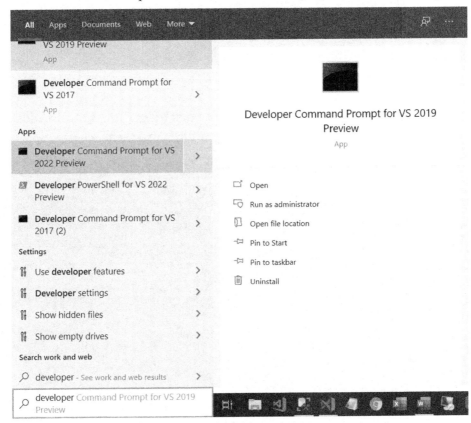

Figure 2.1: Developer Command Prompt for Visual Studio 2022

3. Right click on the **Developer Command Prompt for VS 2022** and select **Run as Administrator**. This provides full access to install the workloads.

4. Type in the following command: **dotnet workload search**

   This searches for available workloads to install.

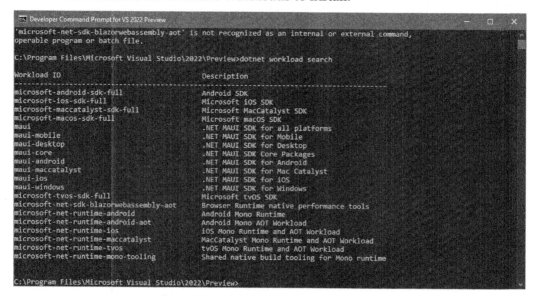

Figure 2.2: Available Workloads

5. Type in the following command: **dotnet workload install maui-desktop**

Figure 2.3: Installing a Workload

6. In the event of an error, it means that the daily workloads aren't published on NuGet.org. This can possibly be solved by editing the **Nuget.config** file with a text string like the following:

```
<add key="maui" value="https://pkgs.dev.azure.com/azure-public/
vside/_packaging/xamarin-impl/nuget/v3/index.json" />
```

Please refer to the *References* section at the end of this chapter for more information regarding NuGet Packages.

.NET SDK: NuGet package validation

.NET includes a new package validation tool that enables NuGet library developers to be able to validate their packages to ensure they are consistent and well-formed. This validation includes:

-   No breaking changes across versions.

-   Same set of public APIs for all runtime-specific implementations.

-   Determine any target-framework- or runtime- applicability gaps.

Validation of packages is crucial to Microsoft's ecosystem. Package validation virtually didn't exist as part of their SDKs and this has caused a lot of headaches for developers. How?

Let's assume that the developer deploys a package that multi-targets for .NET 6.0 and .NET Standard 2.0. There are two different targets to compensate for. The developer must make sure that their code compiled against the .NET Standard 2.0 binary can run against the .NET 6.0 binary.

It can be bit complicated to set up version control, so let's have a closer look with a small exercise:

1. Obviously, the first step is to create a Class Library project that targets .NET Standard or .NET Core, in Visual Studio 2022:

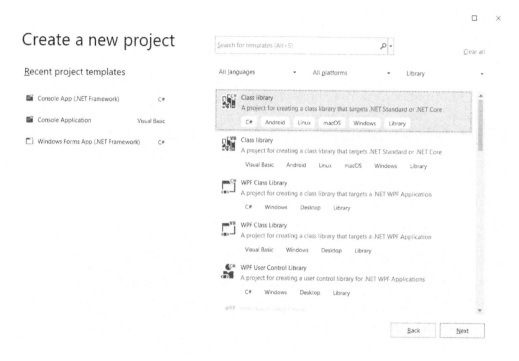

Figure 2.4: *New Class Library Project*

2. Name the project: **PackageValidation_Ex**. This creates the necessary files for our project.

3. Unload the Solution by selecting **File**, **Close Solution** as shown in *Figure 2.5*:

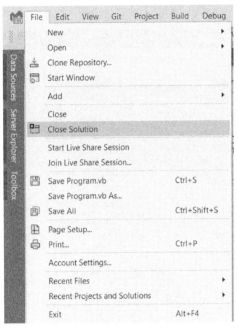

Figure 2.5: *Close Solution*

4. Navigate the folder where the project has been created, then look for the **.csproj** file. This is the project file and is actually editable through Notepad.

5. Right click on the **PackageValidation_Ex.csproj**.

6. Select **Open With** and choose **Notepad**. The file should resemble *Figure 2.6*:

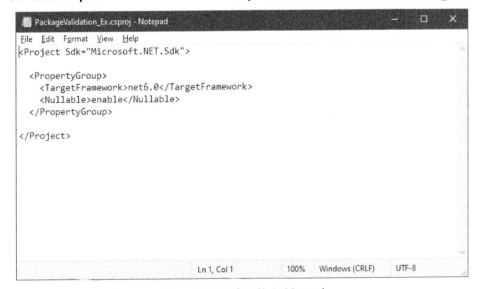

Figure 2.6: *Project file in Notepad*

7. Edit this file to resemble *Figure 2.7*:

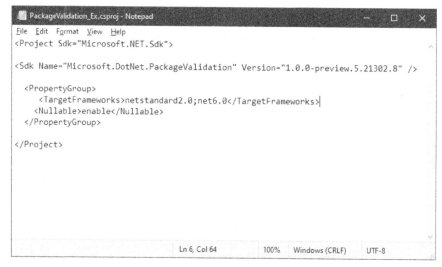

Figure 2.7: *Changed Project file*

Now we can target two projects simultaneously: netstandard2.0 and net6.0.

What next?

We only target the project to two different frameworks, but haven't written code. To demonstrate what will be necessary to cater for both frameworks we need to use preprocessor directives which can compile source code in different environments. Please refer to the *References* section at the end of this chapter for more information regarding preprocessor directives. Here is an example:

```
using System;

namespace PackageValidation_Ex
{
    public class Class1
    {
#if NET6_0_OR_GREATER
    public void MethodThatWorksInNET6AndABOVE()
    {
            // Do something.
    }
#endif
        public void MethodThatDOESNTWorkInNET6AndABOVE(string input)
        {
            // Do something.
```

```
        }
    }
}
```

In this case, we make use of the #if preprocessor directive to determine which framework to use.

Application-wide default font

Although not a .NET 6 feature, but a Visual Studio 2022 feature, the application-wide default font enables programmers to set one font for the entire project. This saves a lot of time. Instead of setting all the controls on all the Windows forms manually, we can now set it only once and it applies to the whole application.

To see this in action, create a new C# Windows Forms App (creating a new application was discussed earlier in this chapter) and name it **DefaultFont_Ex**.

Open the **Program.cs** file by double clicking it in the **Solution Explorer**, as shown in the following Figure:

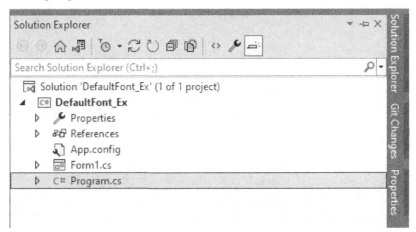

Figure 2.8: Solution Explorer

Edit the main method to look like the following:

```
class Program
{
    [STAThread]
    static void Main()
    {
        Application.EnableVisualStyles();
```

```
    Application.SetHighDpiMode(HighDpiMode.PerMonitorV2);
    Application.SetDefaultFont(new Font(new FontFamily("Microsoft Sans
Serif"), 8f));
    Application.Run(new Form1());
  }
}
```

Fast inner loop

Fast inner loop will make the build run faster, create systems that can skip the build altogether, and enable code edits to be applied to a live process without having to restart it (Hot Reload).

New Math APIs

The **System.Math** namespace in .NET 6 includes new performance-oriented math **Application Programming Interfaces (APIs)**.These new **System.Math** APIs are:

New API	Description	Method Signature
SinCos	Computes Sin and Cos simultaneously	`public (double Sin, double Cos) SinCos(double x);`
ReciprocalEstimate	Computes an approximate of 1 / x	`public static double ReciprocalEstimate (double d);`
ReciprocalSqrtEstimate	Computes an approximate of 1 / Sqrt(x)	`public static double ReciprocalSqrtEstimate (double d);`

Table 2.1: New System.Math APIs

Let's have a look at the .NET 6 enhancements next.

.NET 6 enhancements

.NET 6 includes many exciting improvements and in this section, we will quickly have a look at a few of them.

.NET Multi-platform App UI (.NET MAUI)

.NET Multi-platform App UI is a modern UI toolkit that builds upon and extends Xamarin. With this, we can deliver beautiful and consistent app experiences across various platforms and devices, as well as share more code across mobile and desktop apps. .NET Multi-platform App UI targets Android, iOS, macOS, and Windows.

Not only is the **Xamarin.Forms** toolkit integrated and extended, the **Xamarin. Essentials** library too gets merged into .NET Multi-platform App UI. Using device capabilities and common features are also made easier within .NET Multi-platform App UI.

To create .NET MAUI apps in Visual Studio 2022, we need the following workloads to be installed:

- Mobile development with .NET

- Universal Windows Platform development

- Desktop development with C++

- .NET desktop development

- ASP.NET and web development

This is highlighted in *Figure 2.9:*

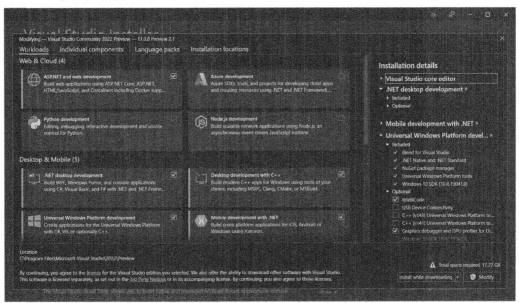

Figure 2.9: .NET MAUI Workloads

After these are installed, a new .NET MAUI application can be created:

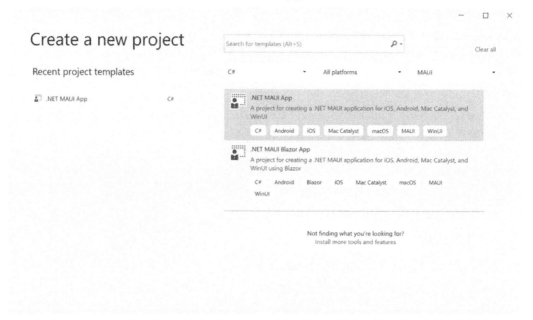

Figure 2.10: *New .Net MAUI App*

The next topic deals with **System.Linq**. If this is an unknown topic, please have a look at the *References* section at the end of this chapter.

System.Linq enhancements

The next table describes the API changes and their possible uses:

API Name	Change	Small Example
Enumerable.Ele-mentAt	It now accepts indices from the end of the enumerable	`Enumerable.Range(1, 5).ElementAt(^2); // returns 4`

TryGetNonEnumer-atedCount	Attempts to obtain the count of the source enumerable without forcing an enumeration	`List<T> buffer = source.TryGetNonEnumeratedCount(out int count) ? new List<T>(capacity: count) : new List<T>();`
		`foreach (T item in source)`
		`{`
		`    buffer.Add(item);`
		`}`

API Name	Change	Small Example
`DistinctBy/` `UnionBy/Inter-` `sectBy/ExceptBy`	Specifies equality using key selector functions	`Enumerable.Range(1, 20).` `DistinctBy(x => x % 3); // {1,` `2, 3}`
`FirstOrDefault/` `LastOrDefault/` `SingleOrDefault`	Returns default(T) if the source enumerable is empty	`Enumerable.Empty<int>().` `SingleOrDefault(999); // returns` `999`

Table 2.2: System.Linq APIs

The last enhancement topic we will cover is Date and Time enhancements.

Date and Time enhancements

.NET exposes DateTime and DateTimeOffset for handling date and time. So, when dealing with only dates or only times some manipulation needs to be done to these methods to extract only a date or only a time. To fix this, or rather compensate for this, .NET 6 now includes structs to cater for only dates only and only times.

DateOnly and TimeOnly structs have the following benefits:

- Each represent either only the date, or only the time.

- **DateOnly** aligns with SQL Server's date type.

- **TimeOnly** aligns with SQL Server's time type.

- Complements existing date/time types including **DateTime**, **DateTimeOffset**, **TimeSpan**, and **TimeZoneInfo**.

Another problem that has been present in .NET is the fact that .NET reads the PC's time zone data from the Windows Registry. For more information on the Windows Registry, please refer to the *References* section at the end of this chapter. Why is this a problem?

Attempting to create a TimeZoneInfo using **Internet Assigned Numbers Authority** (**IANA**) time zone IDs on Windows fail because .NET doesn't have any source of getting such IANA IDs to map to Windows IDS. This also happens with Linux and OSX, because time zone data is read from the installed time zone package that only includes IANA time zone IDs. Attempting to create a TimeZoneInfo using Windows IDs will fail.

The benefits of making use of IANA time zones include the following:

- Implicit conversion when using **TimeZoneInfo.FindSystemTimeZoneById**.

- Explicit conversion through new APIs on **TimeZoneInfo**: **TryConvert IanaIdToWindowsId**, **TryConvertWindowsIdToIanaId**, and **HasIanaId**.

- Improves cross-platform support and interop between systems that use different time zone types.

Conclusion

This chapter gave a quick overview of .NET Framework 6. We delved into the history of the .NET Framework, and had a look at its new and enhanced features.

In *Chapter 3, C# 9 Language & Coding Changes*, we will have a look at all the changes and enhancements to C# in Visual Studio 2022.

Key topics

The common language runtime acts as a virtual agent that manages code at execution time.

Blazor is a framework on which to build interactive client-side web User Interfaces.

.NET APIs include classes, interfaces, delegates, and value types.

.NET includes a new Package Validation tool that enables NuGet library developers to be able to validate their packages to ensure they are consistent and well-formed.

Questions

1. Explain the term .NET MAUI.
2. What does the new SinCos System.Math API do?.
3. Can we target two projects at the same time?

Answers

1. .NET Multi-platform App UI is a modern UI toolkit that builds upon and extends Xamarin.
2. Computes Sin and Cos simultaneously.
3. Yes, netstandard2.0 and net6.0.

References

- **Unmanaged code vs Managed code: https://dotnettutorials.net/lesson/ managed-and-unmanaged-code/**

- CTS: https://docs.microsoft.com/en-us/dotnet/standard/base-types/common-type-system

- Common Intermediate Language: https://dotnettutorials.net/lesson/intermediate-language/

- JIT: https://docs.microsoft.com/en-us/visualstudio/debugger/debug-using-the-just-in-time-debugger?view=vs-2019

- Common Language Specification: https://dotnettutorials.net/lesson/common-language-specification/

- Blazor: https://dotnet.microsoft.com/apps/aspnet/web-apps/blazor

- Preprocessor Directives: https://docs.microsoft.com/en-us/cpp/preprocessor/preprocessor-directives?view=msvc-160

- NuGet Packages: https://www.nuget.org/

- System.Linq: https://docs.microsoft.com/en-us/dotnet/api/system.linq

- Windows Registry: https://docs.microsoft.com/en-us/troubleshoot/windows-server/performance/windows-registry-advanced-users

- IANA: https://www.iana.org/about

CHAPTER 3
Language and Coding Changes in C#

Introduction

The C# language has been around for a very long time and has been evolving over the years. Now, with the advent of newer technologies such as IoT the language had to adapt and grow to compensate for newer platforms.

But, in order to adapt with the C# language, we have to ensure that first, we know the basics of the language, and then, second, see what all the new features can do. This chapter explores the C# language as well as looks at its new features.

Structure

We will cover the following topics:

- C# 9.0
- Variables and Constants
- Datatypes
- Arrays and collections
- Enums

- Selection statements

- Iteration statements

- Source code generator support

- Top-level statements

Objectives

The objective of this chapter is to first: make sure your C# skills are up to date, second: learn the new tricks of C# 9.0, and lastly see where all the new changes fit in and how to practically use them. We will explore various statements such as conditional and iteration statements and the data types.

The C# language

C# has come a long way since being shipped with the first version of the .NET Framework in the year 2000. Originally named **C-like Object Oriented Language (Cool)**, C# has morphed into one of the most popular and powerful programming languages in the world.

We need to understand what makes the language tick, before we can use it productively. Let's explore the common language concepts.

Variables and constants

A variable in programming terms, is a named memory location in which you can store information. This information can be words (strings), whole numbers (integers), decimal numbers (floats), dates, yes / no values (Boolean), and so on. We will go into detail on data types a bit later.

A variable gets its value through process called assignment and it looks like the next statement:

```
VariableName1 = Value;
```

Examples:

```
VariableName2 = 2;
```

```
VariableName3 = "Hello!";
```

VariableName2 now contains a value of 2 and **VariableName3** contains the string **Hello!**

The values stored inside variables can be changed at any time. For example, the value inside the **VariableName2** variable can be changed to 50, or 100 or even 10000.

A constant's value cannot change after it has been assigned a value. Perfect examples of constants are:

Constant	Value
The number of months in a year	12
Minutes in an Hour	60
Seconds in an Hour	3600
Days in a Week	7
Number of Seasons in a Year	4

Table 3.1: *Constants*

Whenever there is a value that might be repeated throughout code, it is always a good idea to convert that value into a constant.

Datatypes

A data type, as the name implies, describes the type of data that can be stored inside a variable or a constant. Without designating a data type, you cannot create a variable. The data type also determines how much space in memory to set aside for a variable or a constant. Earlier in this chapter (in the *Variables and Constants* section) we spoke about strings, Booleans, integers, and floats. These are just some of the few data types the C# language has.

The following table explains the type of values that can be stored as well as the size and range in memory the variable or constant will occupy.

Data Type	Size in Memory	Value
Boolean	Depends on implementing platform	True or False
Byte	1 byte	0 through 255
Char	2 bytes	Codepoints 0 through 65535
Date	8 bytes	0:00:00 AM on January 1, 0001 through 11:59:59 PM on December 31, 9999
Decimal	16 bytes	0 through +/- 79,228,162,514,264,337,593,543,950,335 (+/-7.9...E+28) with no decimal point. 0 through +/- 7.9228162514264337593543950335 with 28 places to the right of the decimal

Data Type	Size in Memory	Value
Double (double-precision floating-point)	8 bytes	-1.79769313486231570E+308 through -4.94065645841246544E-324 for negative values
		4.94065645841246544E-324 through 1.79769313486231570E+308 for positive values
Integer	4 bytes	-2,147,483,648 through 2,147,483,647
Long (long integer)	8 bytes	-9,223,372,036,854,775,808 through 9,223,372,036,854,775,807
Object	4 bytes on 32-bit platform. 8 bytes on 64-bit platform	Any type can be stored in a variable of type Object
SByte	1 byte	-128 through 127
Short (short integer)	2 bytes	-32,768 through 32,767
Single (single-precision floating-point)	4 bytes	-3.4028235E+38 through -1.401298E-45 for negative values. 1.401298E-45 through 3.4028235E+38 for positive values
String (variable-length)	Depends on implementing platform	0 to approximately 2 billion Unicode characters
UInteger	4 bytes	0 through 4,294,967,295
ULong	8 bytes	0 through 18,446,744,073,709,551,615
UShort	2 bytes	0 through 65,535

Table 3.2: Data Types

Creating / declaring variables

In order to create a variable or constant and provide the necessary space in memory for it, we need to declare it. We do it by supplying the data type first, then a decent name, and then optionally an initial value (known as initialising a variable or constant). Here is an example:

```
int Age;
```

The above code creates an integer variable named Age. Let's take the example further:

```
int Age = 40;
```

The above code creates the same variable, but also gives it a starting value of 40. Age is a variable because its value can change. However, when we create a constant, its value cannot change during the course of the program. Here is an example:

```
const string FirstName;

const string LastName;

FirstName = "Ockert";

LastName = "du Preez";
```

Two constants are created in the above code segment, and values populated inside them. These values cannot change while the program is running. The moment you try to assign a new value to a constant, an error will be thrown.

Naming conventions

When naming an object, keep in mind that you are not allowed to use special characters or symbols in the object's name. Also, remember that names cannot start with a number. In general, there are two rules for capitalization in names. These are:

- camelCase
- PascalCase

With camelCasing, the first letter of an object or variable or constant starts with a small letter and every subsequent word in the name starts with a capital letter. With PascalCasing, the name starts with a capital letter and every subsequent word also has a capital letter. Needless to say: names are not allowed to contain spaces.

Arrays and collections

Arrays and collections are known as grouping structures. Both arrays and collections are capable of holding more than one value; the difference comes in, how we want to make use of these values, and how we want to refer them.

Arrays

An array can hold multiple variables of the same type. These variables should be logically related to each other. The individual items of an array are called elements.

Each array element has an index which starts at 0 and ends at the highest element index value. Examples follows next.

Declare a single-dimensional array and populate it with values, as follows:

```
int[] ArrayName1 = new int[5];

    ArrayName1[0] = 0;

    ArrayName1[1] = 1;

    ArrayName1[2] = 1;

    ArrayName1[3] = 2;

    ArrayName1[4] = 3;
```

You can declare and set array element values populated with the first 5 Fibonacci numbers, as follows:

```
int[] ArrayName2 = new int[] { 0, 1, 1, 2, 3 };
```

Alternative syntax to set array element values with the first 10 Fibonacci numbers is shown here:

```
int[] ArrayName3 = { 0, 1, 1, 2, 3, 5, 8, 13, 21, 34, 55 };
```

The Fibonacci sequence in mathematics is when the next number is the sum of the previous two numbers.

Collections

Another way to manage a group of similar information is by making use of Collections. Arrays are usually the best option for creating and working with a fixed number of strongly typed objects, however, Collections are more flexible. Collections can grow and shrink dynamically as the needs of the application change. For the most common collections (such as the Hashtable Class), we can assign a key to any object that was put into the collection so that we can quickly retrieve the object by using the key.

The following classes form part of the Collections Namespace:

- ArrayList
- BitArray
- CaseInsensitiveComparer
- CaseInsensitiveHashCodeProvider
- CollectionBase

- Comparer
- DictionaryBase
- Hashtable
- Queue
- ReadOnlyCollectionBase
- SortedList
- Stack
- StructuralComparisons

Queues

When visiting a bank, a grocery store, or a fast food take away, we have to wait in a queue for service. The .NET queue class replicates this behaviour in memory. The Queue class is what is known as a **First in, first out (FIFO)** list. This means that the first person in the queue will be helped first, and the last person will be helped last. With the items inside a Queue, the first item in the queue will be processed first, and the last will be processed at the end.

We can store values inside a Queue by creating a **Queue** object and using its **Enqueue** method as follows:

```
private Queue MyQueue = new Queue();
private void Button1_Click(object sender, EventArgs e)
      {
              MyQueue.Enqueue("Item 1");
              MyQueue.Enqueue("Item 2");
              MyQueue.Enqueue("Item 3");
      }
```

We can remove items from a Queue by looping through the **Queue** object and using its **Dequeue** method:

```
      private void Button1_Click(object sender, EventArgs e)
      {
         while (MyQueue.Count > 0) {
           object obj = MyQueue.Dequeue;
           Console.WriteLine("from Queue: {0}", obj);
      }
```

Stack

The .NET Stack class can be compared to a stack of vinyl records, or books, or papers on top of each other on a desk. A Stack processes the last item first, and the first item in the stack, last. This is what makes it a **Last in, First out** (**LIFO**) List.

We can store values inside a Stack by creating a **Stack** object and using its **Push** method:

```
private Stack MyStack = new Stack();
    private void Button2_Click(object sender, EventArgs e)
    {
            MyStack.Push("Item 1");
            MyStack.Push("Item 2");
            MyStack.Push("Item 3");
    }
```

We can remove items from a Stack by looping through the **Stack** object and using its **Pop** method:

```
    private void Button2_Click(object sender, EventArgs e)
    {
            while (MyStack.Count > 0) {
        object obj = MyStack.Pop;
        Console.WriteLine("from Stack: {0}", obj);
    }
    }
```

Hashtable

The **Hashtable** collection class enables us to store a collection of information that relates to a certain key. It is a collection of key and value pairs that gets organized based on the hash code of each key.

We can store values inside a Hashtable by creating a **Hashtable** object and giving each item a value:

```
    private Hashtable MyHashtable = new Hashtable();
    private void Button3_Click(object sender, EventArgs e)
    {
            MyHashtable("0") = "Item 1";
            MyHashtable("1") = "Item 2";
            MyHashtable("2") = "Item 3";
    }
```

Loop through the Hashtable by iterating through each **DictionaryEntry** object in the Hashtable:

```
private void Button3_Click(object sender, EventArgs e)
{
    foreach (DictionaryEntry entry in MyHashtable)
    {
        Console.WriteLine("{0} = {1}", pair.Key, pair.Value);
    }
}
```

Enums

An Enumeration is a list of named constants.

Create an Enumeration by using the **enum** keyword shown as follows:

```
enum Day {
    Sunday = 0,
    Monday = 1,
    Tuesday = 2,
    Wednesday = 3,
    Thursday = 4,
    Friday = 5,
    Saturday = 6
};
```

Make use of an enum by optionally creating a new variable and set it to the desired Enum item. Also ensure that the correct data types and the necessary conversions are used, otherwise an error would occur. In the code segment below the variable **FirstDay** is set to the value of Sunday inside the Day Enumeration. This equals 0. LastDay equals 6. Because we are dealing with whole numbers here, we have to cast the enumeration value to the correct data type in order to be stored inside the variables.

An example of Casting variables to the correct data type follows:

```
private void Button4_Click(object sender, EventArgs e)
{
        int FirstDay = (int)Day.Sunday;
        int LastDay = (int)Day.Saturday;
        Console.WriteLine("Sunday = {0}", x);
```

```
                    Console.WriteLine("Saturday = {0}", y);
        }
```

Selection statements

A selection statement causes the program control flow to change depending on whether a certain condition is true or false. The condition is the value we test for. We will briefly examine the **If** statements as well as the switch statement.

If

An **If** statement determines which statement to run based on the value of a Boolean (true / false) expression.

In the following example, the **If** statement tests the value of the **Age** variable. If Age is equal to or greater than 40, a message will be displayed stating **"Old!"**. In case the value is smaller than 40 a message will be displayed stating **"Young!"**

```
int Age = 40;
if (Age >= 40)
{
    MessageBox.Show("Old!");
}
else
{
    MessageBox.Show("Young!");
}
```

In the next example we test for more than one condition – which is the Password, and the program can branch in many different ways. All the passwords supplied in the **else if** statements are valid and will allow entry, whereas in case the **Password** variable doesn't contain any of those values, the else clause kicks in and denies entry.

```
String Password = « BpB » ;
if (Password == « VB.NET »)
{
    MessageBox.Show(« Welcome ! ») ;
}
else if (Password == « C# »)
{
    MessageBox.Show(« Welcome ! ») ;
}
```

```
else if (Password == « .NET »)
{
    MessageBox.Show(« Welcome ! ») ;
}
else if (Password == « BpB »)
{
    MessageBox.Show(« Welcome ! ») ;
}
else if (Password == « OJ »)
{
    MessageBox.Show(« Welcome ! ») ;
}
else
{
    MessageBox.Show(« No Entry ! ») ;
}
```

Switch

The next selection statement is the switch statement. In principle it works the same as an if statement with multiple else if clauses, but it is just simpler and easier to write. Here is the same example as above, but just using a switch statement:

```
string Password = "BpB";
switch (Password)
{
        case "VB.NET":
            MessageBox.Show("Welcome!");
        break;
        case "C#":
            MessageBox.Show("Welcome!");
        break;
        case ".NET":
            MessageBox.Show("Welcome!");
        break;
        case "BpB":
            MessageBox.Show("Welcome!");
        break;
```

```
case "OJ":
    MessageBox.Show("Welcome!");
break;
default:
    MessageBox.Show("No Entry!");
break;
}
```

A lot less typing! Depending on the valid password, entry will be given. If none of the cases match the variable's value, the default clause will step in and display the "**No Entry**" message. We can make this even simpler! Seeing the fact that the same statement has to run if a valid password is supplied, we can do this:

```
switch (Password)
{
    case "VB.NET":
    case "C#":
    case ".NET":
    case "BpB":
    case "OJ":
        MessageBox.Show("Welcome!");
    break;
    default:
        MessageBox.Show("No Entry!");
    break;
}
```

This saves even more time, as we can supply all the conditions, and then the common statement to be run.

Iteration statements

Iteration statements (loops) allow statements inside the loop to be repeated a number of times, or until a certain condition becomes invalid. We can set the number of times the loop should repeat by explicitly stating it (as done with a for next loop), or we can have a condition determine the number of times the loop should repeat (as done with a while loop).

for loop

The for statement executes its inner-statements a number of times, specified in the condition section of the for loop block. An example follows:

```
for (int i = 0; i < 5; i++)
{
    Console.WriteLine(i);
}
```

In the above example the **for loop** is supplied with an initializer, a condition and an iterator. The initializer is the starting point for the loop. As in the example above, an integer variable named i is set to 0. The condition is where i is tested if it is less than 5. If i is any number from 0 to 4 the loop will execute the statement or statements inside the for block. The iterator is the last part where i gets incremented by 1 with the use of the ++ operator.

The for loop, also known as a counter loop, cannot loop more than what was specified, but with the help of the continue, break and throw statements we can exit it early.

foreach loop

The **foreach** statement executes statements for each element in an instance of a type that implements either the **System.Collections.IEnumerable** or the **System. Collections.Generic.IEnumerable<T>** interfaces (such as the Hashtable we spoke about earlier). It sounds more complicated than what it is. Here is a small example:

```
var lstFibonacci = new List<int> { 0, 1, 1, 2, 3, 8, 13, 21, 34, 55 };
foreach (int element in lstFibonacci)
{
    Console.WriteLine($"Element: {element}");
}
```

A list of Fibonacci numbers gets created, and a foreach loop is used to iterate through each of the list's elements to display them in the Console window.

do loop

The do loop executes statements while a specified condition is true, or until the specified condition becomes false. The condition is re-evaluated after each iteration of the do loop. It is very important to remember that a do-while loop executes at least one time regardless whether the condition checked for is true or false. Here is an example:

```
int i = 0;
do
{
    Console.WriteLine(i);
    i++;
} while (i < 5);
```

An integer variable is created. Inside the do loop the value of i gets printed inside the Console window. The value of i gets increased by 1 in each iteration. Lastly, the while condition tests the value of i. Be careful not to create an infinite loop. An infinite loop is a loop that does not exit. Why? Well, because the value being tested never changes. If we removed the part where i gets incremented, this do loop will never exit.

In order to exit a do ; while loop, the goto, return, or throw statements can be used.

while

The while loop executes statements while a specified condition evaluates to true. The condition is evaluated before each execution of the while loop, causing it to execute zero or more times. An example follows:

```
int i = 0;
while (i < 5)
{
    Console.WriteLine(i);
    i++;
}
```

An integer variable named i is created. The test for condition starts the while loop. If the condition is true, the statements inside the loop gets executed. If the condition is initially false (i is equal to or greater than 5) the while loop will never get executed.

We can exit a while loop by using the goto, return, or throw statements.

Source Code Generators Support

In C# 9.0, code generators analyze code and write new source code files as a part of the compilation process, by searching code for attributes and other code elements via the Roslyn analysis APIs. Based on the information received from the APIs, the source generators add code to the compilation. This is the only thing that the code generator may do to the existing code in the compilation.

Some features of source code generators include:

```
Module Initializers
```

Module initializers include the **ModuleInitializerAttribute**, which is used to indicate the compiler that a certain method should be called in the containing module's initializer. A method can include the **[ModuleInitializer]** attribute as shown below.

```
using System;
namespace System.Runtime.CompilerServices
{
    [AttributeUsage(AttributeTargets.Method, AllowMultiple = false)]
    public sealed class ModuleInitializerAttribute : Attribute { }
}
```

The above method can be used as follows.

```
using System.Runtime.CompilerServices;
class clsExample
{
    [ModuleInitializer]
    internal static void mdExample()
    {
        // Code here
    }
}
```

Continuing with the code above, here are a few notes on method initializers :

- They must be declared with static
- The cannot have parameters
- They must return void
- They cannot not be a generic
- They cannot be contained in a generic class

Partial Method Syntax

Partial methods have their signatures defined in one part of a partial types, and their implementations defined in another part of the types. These methods gives the ability to provide method hooks (event handlers) that can be implemented or not, to class designers. If implementation of these methods aren't supplied, the signature of the methods is removed at compile time.

An example follows :

```
namespace PartialMethod_Ex
{
    partial class clsPartialMethod
    {
        partial void MethodToBeCalled(string strTemp);
    }


    //Separate file.
    partial class clsPartialMethod.cs for example
    {
        partial void MethodToBeCalled(String strTemp)
        {
            Console.WriteLine("The Method was called: {0}", s);
        }
    }
}
```

If we were to modify the classes to look like the following, the code would still compile without any issues.

```
namespace PartialMethod_Ex
{
    partial class clsPartialMethod
    {
        partial void MethodToBeCalled(string strTemp);
    }


    //Separate file.
    partial class clsPartialMethod.cs for example
    {
        // partial void MethodToBeCalled(String strTemp)
        //{
            // Console.WriteLine("The Method was called: {0}", s);
        //}
```

```
        }
    }
```

With Partial methods, the declarations must begin with partial and the method signatures must match.

Top-level statements

Everyone who is accustomed to C# should know what the **Program.cs** file looks like, for example. To refresh, an ordinary entry point for your program looks like the following code:

```
using System;
namespace Example_Namespace
{
    class Program
    {
        static void Main(string[] args)
        {
            Console.WriteLine("Hello BpB!");
        }
    }
}
```

This example has the following elements:

- Import of the System namespace

- Namespace declaration

- Program class declaration

- Main method declaration

The **Console.WriteLine** method writes '**Hello BpB!**' to the console. This is the only line of code that actually does something.

With top-level statements we can remove the namespace declaration, class declaration and the method declaration. This looks like the following code:

```
using System;
Console.WriteLine("Hello BpB!");
```

We can write it a step further by removing the using statement as well:

```
Console.WriteLine("Hello BpB!");
```

It is very important to note that only one file is allowed to have top-level statement.

Conclusion

This chapter has taught us a lot, newbies and professionals alike! We have gone through the basics of the C# language where we learned about all the language features in C#. Further on, we had a look at the exciting new features of C#, saw how it can save us time with coding, and learned to implement the new features in our programs.

In the next chapter, we will learn about the new features of .NET Core 3.0. We will see what .NET Framework4.8 can do. Then, we will also learn how to make default executables with .NET Core 3.0 and delve into the Open Source world with WPF, Windows Forms and WinUI.

Questions

1. What is the difference between an Array and a Collection?

2. What is the difference between the for loop and the while loop?

3. Explain the term: Asynchronous Stream?

4. Explain the term Switch Expression?

5. What is the difference between a Variable and a Constant?

Answers

1. Collections can grow dynamically whereas Arrays are not. Collections store values as key / value pairs, and Arrays use indexes.

2. A for loop loops a designated number of times. A while loop loops until a certain condition is false.

3. Await is now able to obtain a stream of results.

4. Switch expressions enable us to use a more concise expression syntax, this means that there are fewer repetitive case and break keywords.

5. Values stored in a Variable can be changed at any time. A Constant's value never change.

CHAPTER 4

Digging into the Visual Studio 2022 IDE

Introduction

The Visual Studio 2022 IDE is the most important tool at our disposal for creating programs. If the IDE is not up to scratch, our programs will not be up to scratch. As simple as that. Knowing how to use the Windows and the tool inside the IDE is crucial in being able to design and code properly.

This chapter explains all the IDE windows and tools and how to use them. Further on, we compare all the IDEs with each other and learn about extensions.

Structure

In this chapter, we will understand the following topics :

- Standard IDE Windows
- Comparing Desktop, Mobile & Web IDEs
- Visual Studio for Mac
- Visual Studio Extensions
- IDE Power Tools

Objectives

After reading this chapter the reader will understand how the normal **Integrated Development Environment** (**IDE**) works and what it does. The reader will also understand the differences between the various platforms that Visual Studio 2022 can be used on to develop various applications specific to the chosen environment. Lastly, we will have a look at some of the power tools that Visual Studio has and what we can do with them.

Standard IDE Windows

The abbreviation IDE means Integrated Development Environment. As the name implies: it is a development environment where you can develop, debug, and deploy any application. Integrated in IDE means that you can develop it in more than one programming language, as Visual Studio is capable of handling languages such as: Visual Basic.NET, C#, F#, JavaScript, and HTML. Visual Studio acts as a proxy for all these languages, a means of building complete modern-day applications, without sacrificing anything from another programming language.

Let's have a look at the standard windows that are available in the Visual Studio 2022 IDE.

Menus

Menus provide access to more features of the IDE. You will find common commands here as well. The beauty of the Visual Studio 2022 IDE: most commands are easily accessible, whether it be through the context menu, built-in menus, toolbars, or keyboard shortcuts.

Toolbars

Toolbars provide quick access to frequently used commands.

Design Window

The design window is usually the first window that gets displayed, depending on the selected project type. If we select a Control Library project upon project creation, there will be no visible designer window as a Control Library doesn't have an interface.

The designer window is where you create the **User Interface** (**UI**) for your project. You add the desired controls from the toolbox onto your form, page, or mobile screen, and set their properties in through the properties window.

In the event of having more than one page, screen, or form, each will be opened in their own tab, thus giving each equal space.

Data sources

In *Chapter 1, Getting started with Visual Studio 2022*, we discussed the **Data Sources** window in brief. We are going to add a Data source now so that we can manipulate information from a database, or even, a file! To see the broader picture, let us add a Data source that connects to an Excel file.

The packages for SQL Server support needs to follow these steps:

1. Start Visual Studio 2022 (as explained in *Chapter 1, Getting to Know the Visual Studio 2022 IDE*) as an Administrator and create a new Desktop C# application. Once that is done, follow the next steps:

2. Open the **Data Sources** window. It is usually located on the left side of the screen, as shown in *Figure 4.1*:

Figure 4.1: Data Sources window

3. Click on **Add New Data Source**. The **Add Data Source Configuration Wizard** dialog window will appear, as shown in *figure 4.2*:

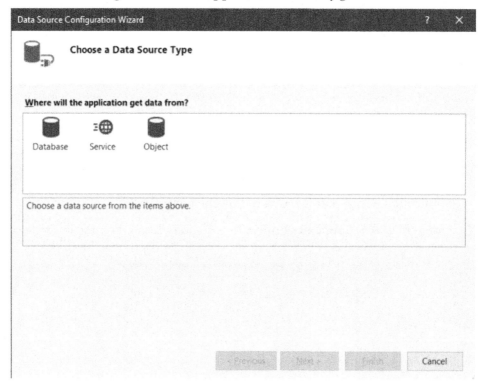

Figure 4.2: *Add Data Source*

4. Select Database and click **Next**. It is important to understand that any file (well, most), if configured correctly can be used as a database. A database such as Microsoft Access or Microsoft SQL Server is known as Relational databases. The reason for this is because all objects in the database is related, for example an Employee database table can be related to a Pension Fund table. There are common items that can be used to link the related items.

> **Note: Flat databases are usually files with content that can be read and manipulated, but it is in a flat structure.**

5. Select **Dataset** from the next screen. *Figure 4.3* displays the Dataset screen:

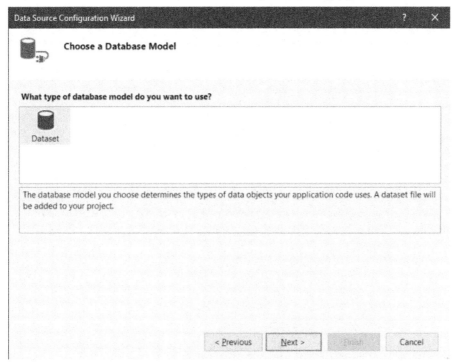

Figure 4.3: *Dataset*

A Dataset is a set of data. The purpose of a Dataset is to hold whatever data was supplied. This gives us the opportunity to make use of the data in any of our programs on any of the platforms.

Obviously, we haven't supplied the Database details or the Dataset details. This is what the next step is for, *Adding a Data Connection*:

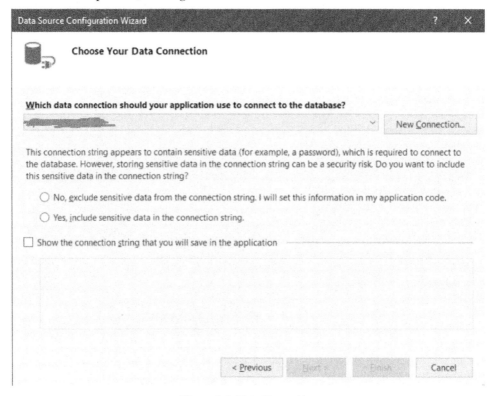

Figure 4.4: *Data Connection*

A Data Connection as the name implies, is a connection to a database. In this case we have to supply the server - where the database is located, the database name and the tables, views, or queries from which the data will come. In our case, we will be adding a file as a database, as we need to keep things easy at this stage. Later in the book we will be doing more advanced data connections and tasks.

1. To add a data connection, click **New Connection**. *Figure 4.5* shows the Choose data Source Window after the '**<other>**' option and a Data Provider have been selected:

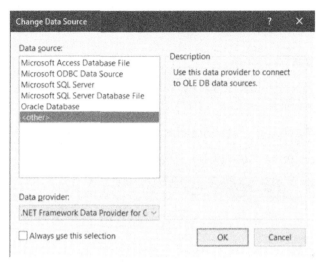

Figure 4.5: *Choose Data Source*

2. A Data Provider is a provider of data. This means it is the technology allowing us to access the desired data source. In this case: .NET Framework Data Provider for **Open Database Connectivity (ODBC)**.

3. Click **Continue**. The next screen appears. In this screen we can select if we want to make use of Access or Excel. *Figure 4.6* shows the selection options:

Figure 4.6: *Excel Connection String*

4. We can connect an Excel file by Selecting the **Use connection string** radio button.

5. Click the **Build** button.

6. Highlight Excel Files (if necessary) and select **New** which will take us to a dialog box where we can select our desired Excel file as a data source.

7. Select the **Machine Data Source** tab and select **New**.

8. Select **User Data Source**, and click **Next**.

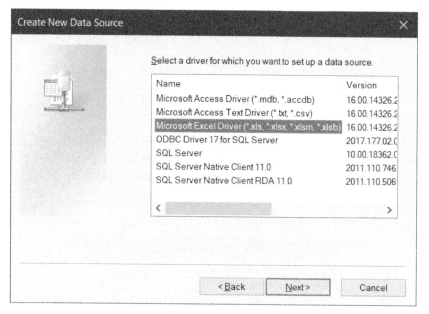

Figure 4.7: Create New Data Source

9. Select the Excel driver, as displayed in *Figure 4.7*.

10. Click **Next**, and then click **Finish**.

11. Name the Data source and give a description.

12. Click **Select Workbook**. Select the desired workbook in the displayed dialog boxes (which still look like Windows 3.1 dialog boxes – beats my why Microsoft haven't upgraded them as well…)

13. Click **OK** twice. This will bring you back to the Add Connection box again.

14. Click **Use user or system data source name**.

15. Click **Refresh**.

16. Select the data source that was added and click **OK**.

17. Click **Next** twice, and then **Finish**.

18. The data source now appears in the Data Sources Window.

Figure 4.8: Added Data Source

After a few simple steps, our **ODBC** Setup displays the Excel file we have selected, in the example: a file named **James Bond.xls** was selected.

Toolbox

The Toolbox is probably the most important window at our disposal in Visual Studio 2022 IDE. The Toolbox is used to add controls to the windows forms, mobile screens, or web pages. It is quite simple to add a control; we can simply double click on the desired control, and it will get added to the form, page, or mobile screen. We can also simply drag a control from the toolbox to the form, or page or mobile screen.

Team Explorer / Git Changes

The Team Explorer window enables us to coordinate our code with other team members while working on a big software project. The Team Explorer window also allows us to manage work which was assigned to single team members, the whole team, or certain projects.

Changes in code that were done during a period of time can be checked in, thus becoming part of the final solution. Upon checking code files, we can select which files to submit and which we are still working on. *Figure 4.9* shows a team explorer window:

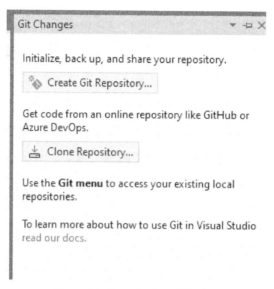

Figure 4.9*: Team Explorer Window*

Notifications

As the name implies, the **Notifications** window displays important notifications (such as important Updates to Visual Studio 2022) from Microsoft concerning Visual Studio 2022. *Figure 4.10* shows what the notification window looks like:

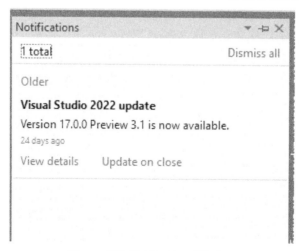

Figure 4.10*: Notifications Window*

Resource view

The Resource view window can be found when the **View** menu is clicked, and then **Other** Windows is selected. It displays all the project's resources. Now, what are resources? A resource is an item that can be added to the project, for example: pictures, files, and strings. These resources can be shipped with the project. To add a resource, open the Project's **Properties** window by following these steps:

1. Click the Project Menu item.

2. Select **Project Name** (this is the project's name) **Properties**.

3. Select the **Resources** tab.

4. Select the type of resource to be added (Image, string, file). These resources can be seen in *Figure 4.11*:

Figure 4.11: Resources

JSON outline

The JSON outline window displays the outline structure of a **JavaScript Object Notation (JSON)** file. JSON is a format in which data gets sent from websites or mobile devices. It is very compact and has a small size, making it the optimal choice of transmitting data. A small example follows:

```
{
    "FirstName": "Ockert",
    "LastName": "du Preez",
    "Gender": "Male",
    "Age": 40,
}
```

On the left-hand-side are the settings and, on the right,-hand-side are the values.

Project properties window

This window enables you to set project wide settings. We have seen earlier how to add resources to our projects, but that is not all we can do. On the **Application** tab we can set the name of the program and the target .NET Framework.

With the Build page we set project Build settings. **Signing** allows us to add certificates to our project, and **Publish** allows us to set publishing settings, especially for our Web Applications.

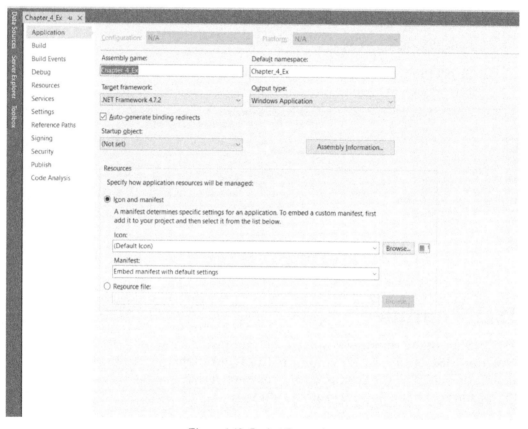

Figure 4.12: *Project Properties*

Add reference window

A reference is an external library we want to make use of in our project. This library can be self-built, or Microsoft supplied, or from any other third party. We add references to our projects by following these steps:

1. Select the **Projects** menu.

2. Click **Add reference**.

3. Or, we can right click on the **Solution Explorer** and select **Add Reference**.

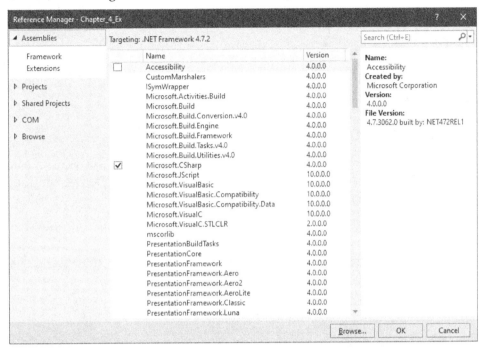

Figure 4.13: Reference

Code window

In *Chapter 1, Getting to Know the Visual Studio 2022 IDE*, we discussed the Code Window in brief, however, now we will dig a bit deeper. As we know, the code window allows us to add the source code to our particular objects and their respective events. *Figure 4.14* shows three aspects of the coding window. These dropdowns help us navigate through our code:

Figure 4.14: Coding Window Navigation

The left-most dropdown shows the projects a certain coding file belongs to, the middle dropdown box displays the classes in the current file and the right-most dropdown displays the events.

Debugging windows

Most debugging windows only appear when the project is running unless they are docked to the side of the IDE. The most common debugging windows are as follows:

- Output window
- Quick watch window
- Locals window

Note: Some Debug windows may only be available during the process of debugging

Output window

The output window is very useful in determining what an object's current value is. When a breakpoint is set, and the IDE enters debugging mode, we can quickly display a value using the **Console.WriteLine** command.

The current value of the object (i) is 23, as shown at the bottom of the Output Window, in *figure 4.15*:

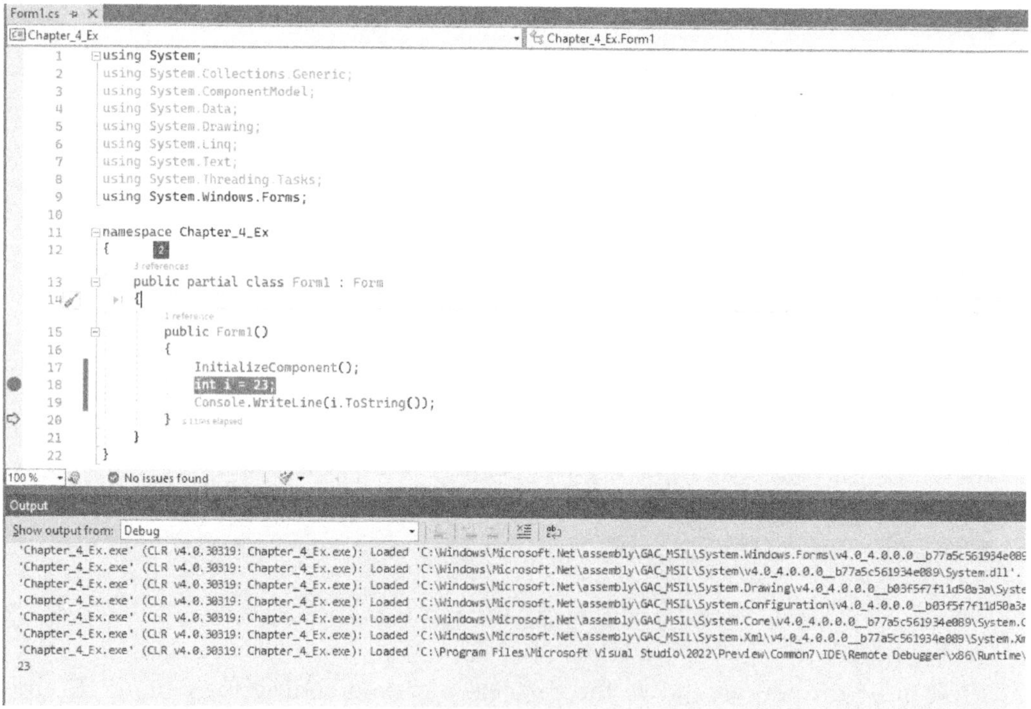

Figure 4.15: Output window

Quick Watch

The benefit of the Quick Watch (found when clicking **Debug**, **Quick Watch**) window is that we do not need extra effort or input in order to determine an object's value. We simply need to set a break point, highlight the object to identify by selecting it using the mouse, then open the Quick Watch window. The value of i is 23 as shown in *Figure 4.16*:

Figure 4.16: *Quick Watch*

Locals

The Locals window is similar to the Quick Watch window, but the nice thing is that it is not a separate dialog box, it can be docked as one of the IDE windows to see results quicker and easier. Access the Locals window by clicking **Debug**, **Windows** | **Locals**.

```
10
11    namespace Chapter_4_Ex
12    {
        3 references
13        public partial class Form1 : Form
14        {
            1 reference
15            public Form1()
16            {
17                InitializeComponent();
18                int i = 23;
19                Console.WriteLine(i.ToString());   ≤ 1ms elapsed
20            }
21        }
22    }
23
```

Name	Value
▶ this	{Chapter_4_Ex.Form1, Text: Form1}
i	23

Figure 4.17: *Locals Window*

Tasks List

The Task List window (**View**, **Task List**) displays all the inactive or incomplete tasks. If we have the following code segment:

```csharp
private void Button1_Click(object sender, EventArgs e)
{
    //UNDONE: Complete this procedure
    int I = 22;
    //TODO: Decrement I value
    i++;
    //HACK: Display value in MessageBox
    Console.WriteLine(i.ToString());
}
```

The **TODO**, **HACK**, and **UNDONE** tokens will display in the **Task List** window, else right click inside the **Task List** window to create any task.

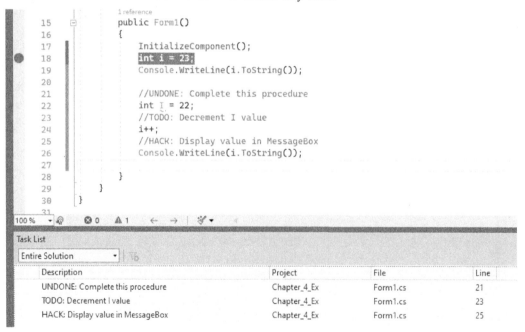

Figure 4.18: Task List Window

The Task List window displays the tasks that need to be done, the name of the project, the file name, as well as the line number.

Comparing desktop, mobile and web IDEs

Most of the IDE's windows still function the same and there is not much difference for each project. For example: the Solution Explorer window will simply display different files and folders, depending on the project type where a big difference in the IDEs can be seen is the Toolbox. Different platforms require different tools.

For each platform, the toolbox is divided into different sections:

Windows Forms

Windows Forms provides a **Graphical User Interface (GUI)** and allows us to write rich client applications for desktop, laptop, and tablet PCs. In order to design the GUI, we need tools specific to the Windows Forms platform, as follows:

- **All Windows Forms**: This Toolbox section holds all Windows related controls, such as buttons, FolderBrowsers, Textboxes, and Labels.

- **Common Controls**: Common Controls are the controls that are most frequently used in Windows Forms projects. These include PictureBoxes, RadioButtons, ListBoxes and CheckBoxes.

- **Containers**: Container controls can host child controls. GroupBoxes and Panels are perfect examples as they can contain any controls inside it, and act like their parent.

- **Menus & Toolbars**: Contains ContextMenuStrip, StatusStrip and ToolStrip controls.

- **Data**: Data Controls include Dataset, DataGridView and Chart.

- **Components**: These are special controls that usually do not have a visible interface, as they work in the background, and remain unseen. These controls include: BackgroundWorker, ImageList, ErrorProvider and Timer.

- **Printing**: Printing controls.

- **Dialogs**: Common Dialog controls such as FontDialog, SaveFileDialog and ColorDialog.

ASP.NET

ASP.NET is a server-side web application framework. Since we will create web applications, we cannot make use of controls designed specifically for Windows. We need proper controls which will enable us to build content rich web applications. The ASP.NET Toolbox are divided into different sections to help finding the right controls faster.

- **Standard**: The Standard section in the ASP.NET Toolbox includes most of the tools that can be used to create decent web applications. These controls include AdRotator, Hyperlink, Button and FileUpload.

- **Data**: Controls to work with and manipulate data. DataList, GridView, DetailsView and SqlDataSource are examples.

- **Validation**: Validation controls help with ensuring entered data is correct. These include RangeValidator and RequiredFieldValidator.

- **Navigation**: Navigation controls include Menu and SiteMapPath.

- **Login**: Login related controls such as Login, PasswordRecovery and CreateUserWizard.

- **WebParts**: Include server widgets such as CatalogZone, EditorZone

- **AJAX Extensions**: Enables us to work with AJAX

- **HTML** : Standard HTML controls such as: Textarea, Select and the Input controls

Xamarin.Forms (Mobile)

In order to create powerful Xamarin apps, the Xamarin Toolbox supplies us with layouts, controls and cells. The layouts are used to structure content on the pages and to host controls, below is a breakdown of the Xamarin Toolbox.

- **Controls**: In the Controls section of the Mobile Toolbox, we find all the basic building blocks to build a decent mobile application. These controls include Entry, Editor, Picker and TimePicker.

- **Layouts**: Layouts are used to organize and structure our mobile app screens. StackLayout enables us to put controls in a column format, FlexLayout gives us more versatility when designing screens and a ScrollView supplies us with a scrollable view.

- **Cells**: The Cells control section includes: ImageCell, TextCell and EntryCell.

Each of the IDEs has its own flavour, and what better way to explore them, than by doing a few small exercises!

Desktop IDE

In *Chapter 1, Getting to Know the Visual Studio 2022 IDE*, we have learned how to create a new C# project, so after the new C# Windows Forms project has been created, make use of the Toolbox and Properties window to add the following controls to the form, and set their properties.

Table 4.1: Desktop Controls

Control	Property	Value
Label	Text	Username
Label	Text	Password
TextBox	PasswordChar	*
Button	Text	Log In
Button	Text	Cancel
Form	Text	Log In
	Size	300, 155

The design should resemble *Figure 4.19*:

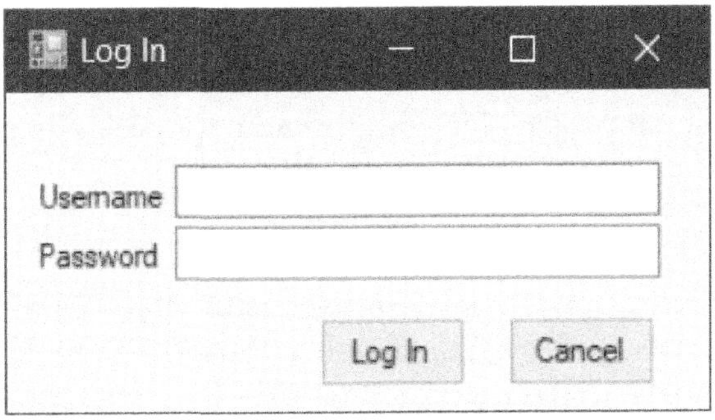

Figure 4.19: Windows Forms

Let us add some code to this very small program:

1. Double click on the '**Log In**' button. Then, add the bold code:

```
private void Button1_Click(object sender, EventArgs e)
{
    if (textBox1.Text == "OJ" && textBox2.Text == "BpB")
    {
        MessageBox.Show("Welcome Back!");
    }
    else
    {
        MessageBox.Show("Try Again.");

    }
}
```

This code checks to what the values are of the two textboxes. If the Username is **OJ** and the Password is **BpB** then a welcoming message will appear, else, a message will appear encouraging the user to try again.

2. Double click on the **Cancel** button, and add the bold code:

```
private void Button2_Click(object sender, EventArgs e)
{
    textBox1.Text = "";
    textBox2.Text = "";
    textBox1.Focus();
}
```

The **Cancel** button clears all the entered text and returns the focus to the first textbox.

Now that we have explored the Windows Desktop Visual Studio IDE with the aid of a small project, let's do the same for a mobile project.

Mobile IDE

When creating a Mobile application, we must ensure that we have installed Xamarin upon installing Visual Studio 2022. Applications that are built using Xamarin contain native user interface controls, so that they look and behave the way the end users expect. Xamarin built apps have access to all the functionality exposed by the underlying device, and can make use of platform-specific hardware acceleration.

Follow these steps to create a mobile application:

1. Create a new Mobile App (Xamarin.Forms) project. Click **Next**.

2. Specify the project's name and location, then click **Create**.

3. In the next box, select **Blank** in the template list and click **OK**.

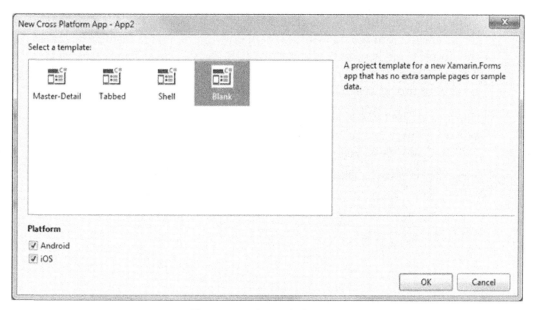

Figure 4.20: Cross Platform App

After the project has been created and finished loading, we will be greeted with a totally different Design IDE.

4. Open the file **MainPage.xaml**.

Notice that coding similar to the following will appear.

```xml
<?xml version="1.0" encoding="utf-8" ?>
<ContentPage xmlns="http://xamarin.com/schemas/2014/forms"
             xmlns:x="http://schemas.microsoft.com/winfx/2009/
xaml"

             xmlns:local="clr-namespace:App2"
             x:Class="MobileLogin.MainPage">


    <StackLayout>
        <!-- Place new controls here -->
        <Label Text="Welcome to Xamarin.Forms!"
           HorizontalOptions="Center"
           VerticalOptions="CenterAndExpand" />
    </StackLayout>


</ContentPage>
```

This is **Extensible Application Markup Language (XAML)**. XAML is a declarative language that describes the design of a page or mobile screen. In the above code segment, the XAML defines a ContentPage. This page will host our current screen content. A StackLayout is used to display a Label control in the centre of the screen.

There is a way to see the design of this page, and that is to click the encircled button shown in the next image. The button beneath it switches back to XAML Code View as shown in *Figure 4.21*:

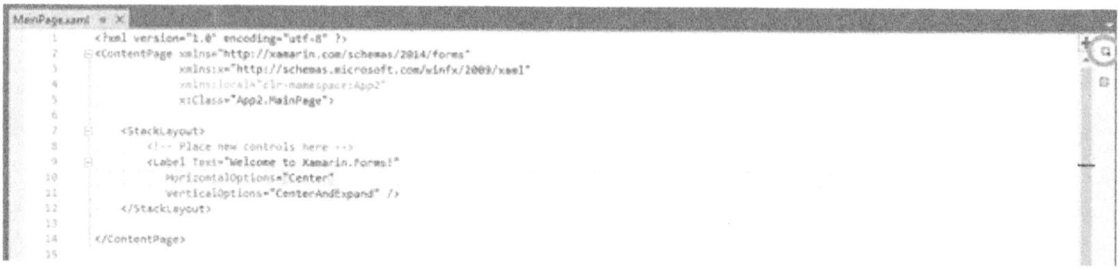

Figure 4.21: XAML Code View

Make use of the Toolbox and Properties window to add the following controls to the form and set their properties.

Control	Property	Value
Label	Text	User Name
Label	Text	Password
Entry	Placeholder	Username
Entry	IsPassword	True
Button	Text	Login
Button	Text	Cancel

Table 4.2: Mobile Controls

We can also add the XAML code manually to add controls to our page. This takes some getting used to, and some learning.

```
<?xml version="1.0" encoding="utf-8" ?>

<ContentPage xmlns="http://xamarin.com/schemas/2014/forms"
            xmlns:x="http://schemas.microsoft.com/winfx/2009/xaml"
            xmlns:local="clr-namespace:MobileLogin"
            x:Class="MobileLogin.MainPage">


    <StackLayout VerticalOptions="StartAndExpand">
```

```
        <Label Text="User Name" />
        <Entry x:Name="usernameEntry" Placeholder="Username" />
        <Label Text="Password" />
        <Entry x:Name="passwordEntry" IsPassword="true" />
        <Button Text="Login" Clicked="OnLoginButtonClicked" />
        <Button Text="Cancel" Clicked="OnCancelButtonClicked" />

        <Label x:Name="messageLabel" />
    </StackLayout>

</ContentPage>
```

The Design should resemble *Figure 4.22*:

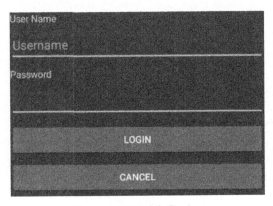

Figure 4.22: *Mobile Design*

Where do we add the code? Well, we still need to add our C# code for these buttons to work. In the Solution Explorer, search for the file named **MainPage.xaml.cs**, then open it by double clicking on it. This is where we add the C# code for these objects.

Add the following bold code for the **Login** button and for the **Cancel** button.

```
void OnLoginButtonClicked(object sender, EventArgs e)
    {

        if (usernameEntry.Text == 'OJ' && passwordEntry.Text == 'BpB')
         {
            messageLabel.Text = "Welcome Back";
         }
```

```
        else
        {
            messageLabel.Text = "Try Again";
        }
    }


    void OnCancelButtonClicked(object sender, EventArgs e)
    {
        usernameEntry.Text = "";
        passwordEntry.Text = "";
        usernameEntry.Focus();
    }
```

The code is basically the same as what we did earlier with the desktop project, except that we display the Welcoming message and '**Try Again**' message inside a label instead of a MessageBox.

Web IDE

To create a Web Application, we need to create an ASP.NET Web Application project. ASP.NET is an open-source web framework for building web applications and services with .NET. After we have selected the **ASP.NET Web Application** project and clicked **Next**, a new screen will appear prompting us to choose the type of ASP.NET Application. These types include:

- **Empty**: This template contains no content.

- **Web Forms (the one we will create)**: This template provides a design surface which we can use to host controls and our content.

- **MVC**: This enables us to create web applications making use of the **Model-View-Controller (MVC)** architecture.

- Web API. This enables us to create **Representational State Transfer (RESTful)** HTTP services.

- **Single Page Application**: This template enables us to create a JavaScript driven HTML5 application with the use of ASP.NET, Web API, CSS3 and JavaScript.

After the new ASP.Net Web Application has been created, double click on one of the pages, such as **Default.aspx**. This is usually the home page of a web application.

We need to get rid of the paragraphs and headings that has been automatically added by the designer by deleting them. Then, after all have been deleted, make use of the Toolbox and Properties window to add the following controls to the form and set their properties.

Control	Property	Value
LogIn	DisplayRememberMe	False
	LoginButtonType	Link

Table 4.3: ASP.NET Controls

The Design should resemble *Figure 4.23*:

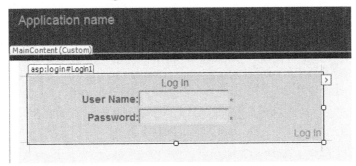

Figure 4.23: Web Login

The Design window is split into three sections:

- Design (which we have been working with)

- **Split**: This View displays the design view as well as the underlining HTML code.

- **Source**: This View shows the HTML code making up your design.

Hypertext Markup Language (HTML) is the language used in order to create Web pages. HTML elements are represented by tags (the elements between the <> signs) which identifies pieces of content such as "heading", "paragraph", "table", "image" etc. The code behind the Login design, looks like the following:

```
<%@ Page Title="Home Page" Language="C#" MasterPageFile="~/Site.Master"
AutoEventWireup="true" CodeBehind="Default.aspx.cs" Inherits="WebLogin._
Default" %>

<asp:Content    ID="BodyContent"    ContentPlaceHolderID="MainContent"
runat="server">

    <div class="jumbotron">
```

```
        <asp:Login ID="Login1" runat="server" DisplayRememberMe="False"
LoginButtonType="Link" RememberMeSet="True" Width="412px">

        </asp:Login>
    </div>

    <div class="row">
        <div class="col-md-4">
        </div>
    </div>

</asp:Content>
```

The Login control is placed inside a **div** element, which is placed inside a **Content** element. For our application to do something, we must add the code in the C# class file. An easy way to do this is to Navigate to the **LoggingIn** event in the **Properties** Window, then double clicking it. Else, we could search for the **.cs** file in the Solution Explorer as we did earlier. Add the code highlighted in bold:

```
        protected void Login1_LoggingIn(object sender, LoginCancelEventArgs e)
        {
            if (Login1.UserName == "OJ" && Login1.Password == "BpB")
            {
                Login1.TitleText = "Welcome Back";


            }
            else
            {
                Login1.TitleText = "Try Again";
                Login1.UserName = "";


            }
        }
```

Although we have worked in three different IDEs on three different platforms, the underlying C# code mostly remains the same. However, this may not always be the case, as this book is showing examples that aren't too complex (yet.)

Visual Studio for Mac

So far, we have spoken a lot about Visual Studio 2022 for use on a Windows Platform. Now, let's discuss Visual Studio for Mac users.

Visual Studio for Mac is being moved to the native macOS UI thus fixing hundreds of previously reported issues. This move also allows the Visual Studio **Integrated Development Environment (IDE)** to work more reliably.

Visual Studio for Mac has a new look and feel that combines the elements of the macOS UI and the productivity of Visual Studio. The menus and user experience in Visual Studio have also been updated.

Git tooling in the Visual Studio IDE has been updated to provide more stability. Part of the improved Git tooling experience is having a new Git Changes window and a new Git Branch selector.

Visual Studio 2022 extensions

Extensions or Add-Ins are code packages that can run inside the Visual Studio 2022 IDE. Extensions provide new or improved Visual Studio features. This can be anything! From improving on scrolling features, to improving the IDE windows. There are literally thousands of Extensions available on the Visual Studio Marketplace: **https://marketplace.visualstudio.com/**

Visual Studio Marketplace is the exclusive place for purchasing and renewing subscriptions, as well as for finding new extensions for Visual Studio and Visual Studio Code. Some extensions are free, whereas some are paid. It all depends on the needs of the development team. Extensions exist so that our productivity can be improved.

For more information on Visual Studio 2022 extensions, please have a look at the *References* section at the end of this chapter.

Let's add some useful extensions to our Visual Studio 2022 IDE.

Finding and installing extensions

You can follow these steps to find and install extensions:

1. Navigate to **https://marketplace.visualstudio.com/**.

2. In the Search bar type in `RockMargin` and press `Enter`, or click on `Search`.

3. The result will be displayed. It shows a brief summary of the Extension.

4. Click on **RockMargin**. This brings us to the download page. It gives a good description and more details on how this extension work.

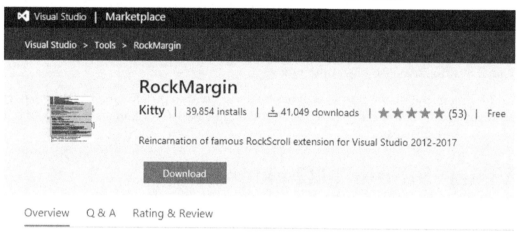

Figure 4.24: RockMargin

5. Select **Download**. The VSIX file will download. The VSIX file is a compressed file holding all the necessary coding files that will extend the functionality of the IDE.

6. Navigate to the file, and double click the VSIX file.

Image optimizer

Follow the same steps to search for an extension called **Image Optimizer** and install it:

Figure 4.25: Image Optimizer

Follow the same procedure and add an Extension named SmartPaster2022.

Note: We can also use the Extensions menu in the Visual Studio 2022 IDE to search for nice Extensions.

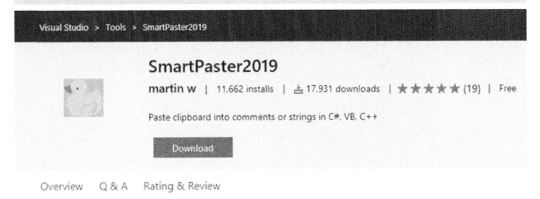

Figure 4.26: SmartPaster

Creating a very basic extension

Visual Studio SDK needs to be installed before you can develop extensions for Visual Studio 2022. It can be installed when Visual Studio 2022 is being installed for the first time, or afterwards.

1. Create a new project and select VSIX as the template.

2. After the project has loaded, right-click the project node in Solution Explorer.

3. Select **Add**, **New Item**.

4. Expand the Extensions node under Visual C#.

5. Choose from the available item templates (For our project, select **Custom Command**, as shown in *Figure 4.26*):

    a) Visual Studio Package

    b) Editor Items

    c) Command

    d) Tool Window

    e) Toolbox Control

6. Click **Add**.

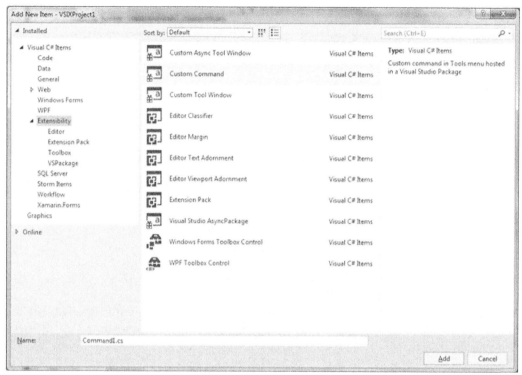

Figure 4.27: Extension

7. Double click the vsct file. The code will open. Make sure to read the comments since they explain what is happening. The vsct file is where we can change the design of the objects and add objects.

8. Change the text of the button to "**Click Me**", as shown in bold.

```xml
<Button guid="guidVSIXProject1PackageCmdSet"
id="Command1Id" priority="0x0100" type="Button">

    <Parent guid="guidVSIXProject1PackageCmdSet"
id="MyMenuGroup" />

    <Icon guid="guidImages" id="bmpPic1" />

    <Strings>

        <ButtonText>Click Me!</ButtonText>

    </Strings>

</Button>

</Buttons>
```

9. Open the **Command1.cs** file and modify the Execute procedure to the following:

```
private void Execute(object sender, EventArgs e)
{
    ThreadHelper.ThrowIfNotOnUIThread();
    string message = "My first Extension";
    string title = "Extension Title";

    // Show a message box to prove we were here
    VsShellUtilities.ShowMessageBox(
        this.package,
        message,
        title,
        OLEMSGICON.OLEMSGICON_INFO,
        OLEMSGBUTTON.OLEMSGBUTTON_OK,
        OLEMSGDEFBUTTON.OLEMSGDEFBUTTON_FIRST);
}
```

10. Run the Extension by clicking on the **Run**/**Start** button inside Visual Studio.

   A new instance of Visual Studio Experimental Instance will be spawned, but remember, this is just for testing the Extension. It still must be installed and published properly.

11. *Figure 4.28* displays the extension listed in the **Tools** menu. On the **Tools** menu, select "**Click Me!**"

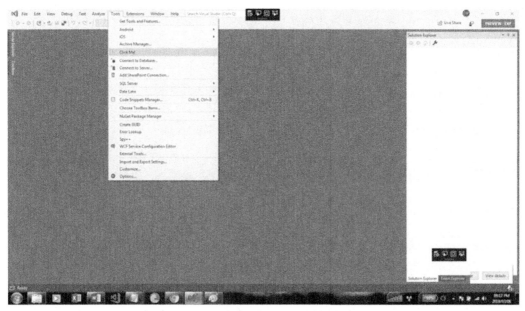

Figure 4.28: Test Extension

12. Click on it. A MessageBox will appear, as shown in *Figure 4.29*:

Figure 4.29: Test Extension Result

IDE Productivity Power Tools

Productivity Power Tools 2022 is an extension bundle installer from Microsoft DevLabs that will install its components individually. It contains the following extensions:

- **Align Assignments**: This Extension enables us to align variable assignments.

- **Copy As Html**: This copies the text in HTML format.

- **Double-Click Maximize**: Maximize and Dock windows.

- **Fix Mixed Tabs**: This fixes tab spacing.

- **Match Margin**: This Extension draws markers on the Visual Studio IDE scrollbars.

- **Middle-Click Scroll**: Allows us to scroll with the help of a Middle Mouse button click.

- **Peek Help**: Shows F1 Help inline in the code editor.

- **Power Commands for Visual Studio**: A set of useful extensions for the IDE.

- **Quick Launch Tasks**: Provides accessibility of frequent tasks.

- **Shrink Empty Lines**: Removes empty lines in the code editor.

- **Solution Error Visualizer**: Highlights errors and warnings inside the Solution Explorer.

- **Time Stamp Margin**: This adds a Time stamp to the debug output window.

Conclusion

In this chapter we were introduced to the Visual Studio 2022 IDE. We learned about the differences between all the IDEs of Visual Studio 2022. We learned about Extensions (What they are and how useful they can be) and how to make them. We also learned about the Productivity Power Tools available.

In the next chapter, we will focus on AI IntelliCode. We will explore the new AI IntelliCode and its AI capabilities to cater for a better coding experience.

Key topics

- Standard IDE Windows

- Project Properties

- Debugging Windows

- Windows Forms

- Cross Platform App

- Visual Studio for Mac

Points to remember

- Extensions or Add-Ins are code packages that can run inside the Visual Studio 2022 IDE.

- Productivity Power Tools 2022 is an extension bundle installer from Microsoft DevLabs that will install its components individually.

- Visual Studio for Mac is being moved to the native macOS UI.

- The Design window is split into three sections.

- Some Debug windows may only be available during the process of debugging

Questions

1. Name three debugging windows.

2. What is the purpose of the Project Properties window?

3. What is the purpose of the Toolbox window?

Answers

1. They are:
   a. Output Window
   b. Quick Watch Window
   c. Locals Window

2. This window enables you to set project wide settings.

3. The Toolbox is used to add controls to the Windows Forms, Mobile screens, or Web pages.

Section - II
Using The Tools in
Visual Studio 2022

This section will include the following chapters:

- AI IntelliCode
- Built-in tools
- Diagnostics and debugging

CHAPTER 5
AI IntelliCode

In order to author proper code, we need proper tools to assist us. Tools such as IntelliSense and IntelliCode not only saves us valuable coding time, but also assists us in conforming to the most popular coding standards.

In this chapter we will learn about IntelliCode: what it is, and its improvements and benefits. Then we move on to explaining artificial intelligence in order to understand IntelliCode better.

Structure

In this chapter we will cover the following topics :

- IntelliSense
- Assisted IntelliSense
- Advantages of using IntelliCode
- Team completions
- Argument completion
- Style and formatting conventions

Objectives

This chapter will teach the ins-and-outs of IntelliSense in Visual Studio 2022. We will learn what IntelliSense is and how to use it. Then, we will learn about Assisted IntelliSense and what the differences are between normal IntelliSense and Assited IntelliSense. The most interesting thing that you will learn in this chapter are team completions and argument completions. Let's start having fun!

IntelliSense

IntelliSense is an IDE tool that completes code, or in better words: it is a code-completion tool that assists us while we are typing our code. IntelliSense helps us add property and method calls using only a few keystrokes, keeps track of the parameters we are typing, and learn more about the code we are busy using. IntelliSense is mostly language specific.

IntelliSense includes the following features:

- **List Members**

  Usually when a trigger character such as a period (.) in managed code such as C# and VB.NET, or double-colon (::) in C++ is pressed, a list of members from a type or namespace appears. As we type, the list filters to provide a proper Camel Case selection. We can make a selection by double-clicking on the provided item or pressing the tab or space button. The member list also provides quick info, meaning that if we hover our mouse over an item, we get an idea of the member's purpose and parameters.

  You can also invoke the List Members feature manually by typing *Ctrl + J*, choosing Edit, IntelliSense, List Members, or by choosing the List Members button on the editor toolbar. To turn List Members on (if it is off) navigate to `Tools` | `Options` | `All Languages` and deselect `Auto list members`.

Figure 5.1 displays a list of String members that we possibly want to use, such as Length (which gives us the length, or rather, the number of characters, of the current string).

Figure 5.1: *List Members*

- **Parameter Info**

  Parameter Info provides us with information on the number, names, or the types of parameters required by a certain method, C++ template or a C# attribute generic type parameter. The bold parameter indicates the next required parameter while we are typing the function. In an overloaded function, we can simply use the Up or Down arrow keys to view different parameter information for the function overloads.

  When functions and parameters are annotated with XML Documentation comments, the comments will display as Parameter Info.

  We can manually invoke Parameter Info by choosing **Edit | IntelliSense | Parameter Info**, by pressing *Ctrl + Shift + Space*, or by choosing the **Parameter Info** button on the editor toolbar.

  Figure 5.2 shows the various Parameters available for the **Console. WriteLine** command. In the example string format, in bold is the current parameter that needs to be the input for the 19th overload.

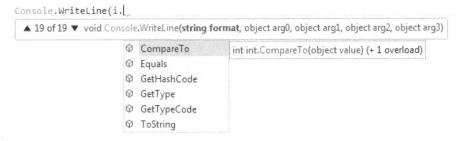

Figure 5.2: *Parameter Info*

- **Quick Info**

  Quick Info displays the complete declaration for any identifier in our code. As mentioned earlier, after we select a member from the List Members box, Quick Info appears.

  We can manually invoke Quick Info by choosing **Edit**, **IntelliSense**, **Quick Info**, or by pressing *Ctrl + I, Ctrl + K*, or by choosing the **Quick Info** button on the editor toolbar.

  Figure 5.3 displays the Quick Info for the **Console** class.

  ```
  Console.WriteLine(i.ToString());
  ```
  <kbd>class System.Console</kbd>

Figure 5.3: *Quick Info*

- **Complete Word**

  Complete Word completes the rest of a command, object, variable, or function name after enough characters have been entered to disambiguate the term.

  We invoke Complete Word by choosing **Edit | IntelliSense | Complete Word**, or by pressing *Ctrl + Space*, or by choosing the **Complete Word** button on the editor toolbar.

  The next image shows IntelliCode in action:

Figure 5.4: *IntelliCode in action*

Template IntelliSense improvements in C++

In C++, a function template defines a family of functions and a class template defines a family of classes. IntelliSense for these Templates were only introduced in Visual Studio 2017 15.8 Preview 3 with the inclusion of the Template Bar.

Peek Window UI and live edits

Peek Window UI allows us to do live edits and it integrates nicely into our workflow. The reason why this is so important is because when we used to click the edit button on the Template bar, a modal box used to pop-up. Because of this, making live changes were impossible and difficult. Now, as we type template arguments, IntelliSense updates it in real time thus enabling us to see how the arguments may affect our code.

Nested template support

The template bar used to only appear at a top-level parent template. Now it includes support for nested templates.

Default argument watermarks

If there is a default argument present, the textbox inside the peek window gets automatically populated with it, otherwise a different argument can be specified.

AI IntelliCode

Artificial Intelligence (AI), or Machine Intelligence is simply put: intelligence demonstrated by machines. This means that we can teach machines to do certain tasks, or program them in a way that they are able to learn things themselves.

Visual Studio IntelliCode makes use of machine learning to offer contextually-rich code completion suggestions as code is being typed. This allows the developer to code faster. IntelliCode's base model was trained on over 3000 top open source C# GitHub repositories with over 100 stars. But with this in mind, we need to note that IntelliCode does not include all the custom types in developers' code bases. In order to produce contextually-rich suggestions, the base model needs to be trained and tailored to unique types that aren't used in open source code and the developer team's code.

IntelliCode saves a developer's time by putting what the developer is most likely to use at the top of his or her completion list. As mentioned above, IntelliCode recommendations are based on thousands of open-source projects on GitHub. This enables promotion of common practices. IntelliCode presents the most relevant overloads first - these are indicated by a star icon. It works the same with a member's signature or overloads that are shown in the IntelliSense tool-tip, plus it will include additional wording to explain the recommended status.

Advantages of using IntelliCode

Using IntelliCode has several advantages such as the following:

- Assisted IntelliSense
- Recommendations for your types, based on your code (C#)
- Inferring code style and formatting conventions
- Finding issues faster
- Focused code reviews

Assisted IntelliSense

As the name implies, Assisted IntelliSense assists the developer with hints and tips on how a certain method works or should be implemented. IntelliCode saves time by putting what we're most likely to use at that particular point in time, at the top of the completion list. This is due to its built-in Artificial Intelligence which follows recommendations based on common practices used by thousands of developers in various open-source projects.

Recommendations for types, based on code

IntelliCode can learn patterns from our code so that it can make recommendations for types that aren't in the open source domain, such as your own utility classes. Do not worry, the service keeps the trained models secured so that it cannot be accessed by those we don't choose to share our models with.

Inferring code style and formatting conventions

Visual Studio IntelliCode dynamically creates an `.editorconfig` file from our codebase to define our coding styles and formats. This will be explained later in this chapter.

Finding issues faster

Finding issues faster by seeing issues in context. IntelliCode automatically scans our code when we commit or review it. Visual Studio IntelliCode makes use of Artificial Intelligence to learn from source code to spot variable misuse, missed refractorings and irregular patterns among others.

Focused code reviews

Visual Studio IntelliCode acts as an extra pair of eyes on our code reviews. It highlights changes which might require more attention based on factors like complexity, churn, and history.

Team completions

IntelliCode provides recommendations based on the currently entered code and seamlessly share these recommendations across the development team. With IntelliCode, developers can build a team model to provide recommendations on code that is not really in the open-source domain, such as specific methods on the developers' own utility classes or domain specific library calls.

Train models for team completions

To train team completions on your repositories, follow these steps:

1. Open the repository with the solution to train on.

2. Agree to the Visual Studio "gold bar" notification asking for consent to train a model for that repository. Else, select **View** | **Other Windows** | **IntelliCode**. This is shown in *figure 5.5* :

Figure 5.5: IntelliCode menu option

3. Check the "**I accept these terms and would like to train IntelliCode models on my currently open codebase: <Solution Name>**" checkbox, as shown in *figure 5.6*:

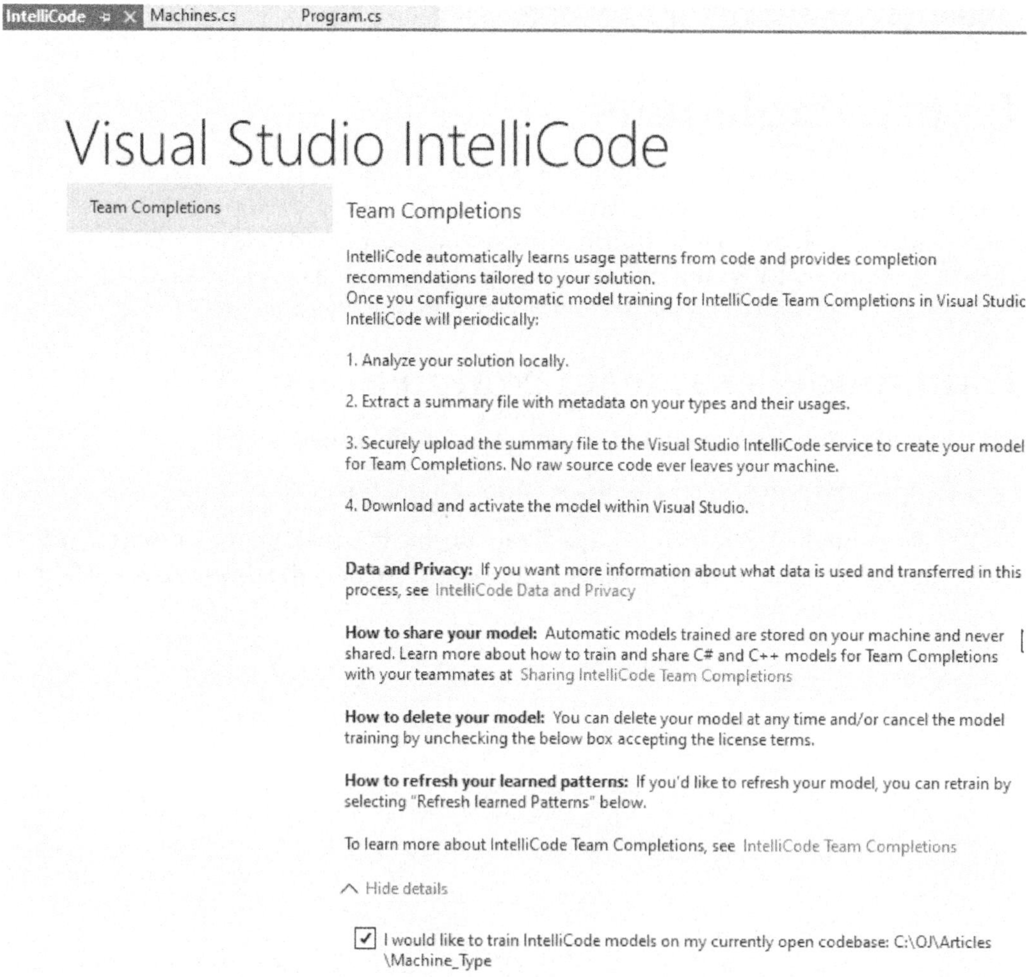

Figure 5.6: Agree to terms

When the model is created successfully, it will be automatically downloaded to Visual Studio.

Argument completion

Besides statement completion signature help, IntelliCode can also make argument recommendations in order to help choose the right argument quickly.

Style and formatting conventions

Visual Studio IntelliCode dynamically creates an **.editorconfig** file from our codebase to define our coding styles and formats.

EditorConfig

An EditorConfig file helps us maintain a consistent coding style while working with multiple developers on the same project with different editors and IDEs. An EditorConfig project consists of a file format that defines coding styles, and plugins that enable editors to read the file format and adhere to defined styles.

Creating an EditorConfig file

To create an editor config file, follow these steps:

1. Right click on the **Solution** in the Solution Explorer.

2. Navigate to **Add**.

3. Select **New EditorConfig**. *Figure 5.7* shows this in action:

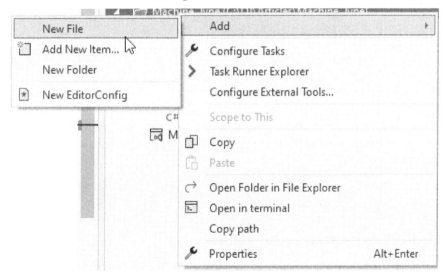

Figure 5.7: Create new EditorConfig

4. Or, follow step 1 and navigate to **Add New Item**.

5. Select editorconfig file (.NET) to add a .NET specific editor config file. This is shown in *Figure 5.8* below :

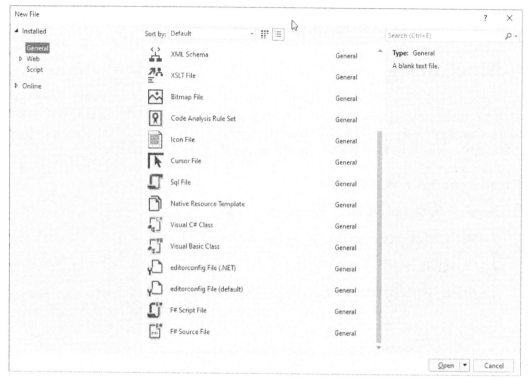

Figure 5.8: New Editor Config file in New File Dialog box

Another option exists. This option allows the developer to generate an **EditorConfig** file from the current Visual Studio Settings, and even change some of the settings first. Follow these steps:

1. Click **Tools**.

2. Click **Options**.

3. Select **Text Editor**.

4. Select the language of choice, in this case C#.

5. Select **Code Style**.

6. Select **General**. This is shown in *Figure 5.9*:

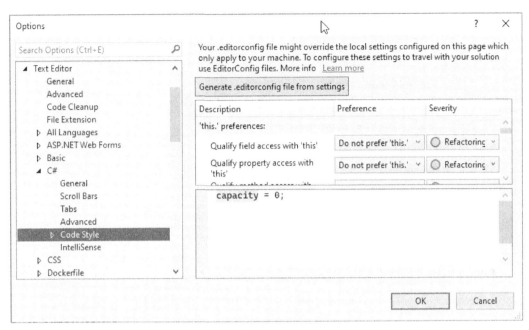

Figure 5.9: *Editor Config Options*

7. The file will display in the code editor. It looks like the following:

```
# To learn more about .editorconfig see https://aka.ms/editorcon-
figdocs
###############################
# Core EditorConfig Options    #
###############################
# All files
[*]
indent_style = space

# XML project files
[*.{csproj,vbproj,vcxproj,vcxproj.filters,proj,projitems,shproj}]
indent_size = 2

# XML config files
[*.{props,targets,ruleset,config,nuspec,resx,vsixmanifest,vsct}]
indent_size = 2

# Code files
[*.{cs,csx,vb,vbx}]
```

```
indent_size = 4
insert_final_newline = true
charset = utf-8-bom
###############################
# .NET Coding Conventions      #
###############################
[*.{cs,vb}]
# Organize usings
dotnet_sort_system_directives_first = true
# this. preferences
dotnet_style_qualification_for_field = false:silent
dotnet_style_qualification_for_property = false:silent
dotnet_style_qualification_for_method = false:silent
dotnet_style_qualification_for_event = false:silent
# Language keywords vs BCL types preferences
dotnet_style_predefined_type_for_locals_parameters_members =
true:silent
dotnet_style_predefined_type_for_member_access = true:silent
# Parentheses preferences
dotnet_style_parentheses_in_arithmetic_binary_operators = always_
for_clarity:silent
dotnet_style_parentheses_in_relational_binary_operators = always_
for_clarity:silent
dotnet_style_parentheses_in_other_binary_operators = always_for_
clarity:silent
dotnet_style_parentheses_in_other_operators = never_if_unneces-
sary:silent
# Modifier preferences
dotnet_style_require_accessibility_modifiers = for_non_interface_
members:silent
dotnet_style_readonly_field = true:suggestion
# Expression-level preferences
dotnet_style_object_initializer = true:suggestion
dotnet_style_collection_initializer = true:suggestion
dotnet_style_explicit_tuple_names = true:suggestion
dotnet_style_null_propagation = true:suggestion
```

```
dotnet_style_coalesce_expression = true:suggestion

dotnet_style_prefer_is_null_check_over_reference_equality_method
= true:silent

dotnet_style_prefer_inferred_tuple_names = true:suggestion

dotnet_style_prefer_inferred_anonymous_type_member_names = true:-
suggestion

dotnet_style_prefer_auto_properties = true:silent

dotnet_style_prefer_conditional_expression_over_assignment =
true:silent

dotnet_style_prefer_conditional_expression_over_return = true:si-
lent

###############################
# Naming Conventions          #
###############################
# Style Definitions
dotnet_naming_style.pascal_case_style.capitalization
= pascal_case
# Use PascalCase for constant fields
dotnet_naming_rule.constant_fields_should_be_pascal_case.severity
= suggestion

dotnet_naming_rule.constant_fields_should_be_pascal_case.symbols
= constant_fields

dotnet_naming_rule.constant_fields_should_be_pascal_case.style
= pascal_case_style

dotnet_naming_symbols.constant_fields.applicable_kinds
= field

dotnet_naming_symbols.constant_fields.applicable_accessibilities
= *

dotnet_naming_symbols.constant_fields.required_modifiers          =
const

###############################
# C# Coding Conventions       #
###############################
[*.cs]
# var preferences
csharp_style_var_for_built_in_types = true:silent
csharp_style_var_when_type_is_apparent = true:silent
```

```
csharp_style_var_elsewhere = true:silent
# Expression-bodied members
csharp_style_expression_bodied_methods = false:silent
csharp_style_expression_bodied_constructors = false:silent
csharp_style_expression_bodied_operators = false:silent
csharp_style_expression_bodied_properties = true:silent
csharp_style_expression_bodied_indexers = true:silent
csharp_style_expression_bodied_accessors = true:silent
# Pattern matching preferences
csharp_style_pattern_matching_over_is_with_cast_check = true:sug-
gestion
csharp_style_pattern_matching_over_as_with_null_check = true:sug-
gestion
# Null-checking preferences
csharp_style_throw_expression = true:suggestion
csharp_style_conditional_delegate_call = true:suggestion
# Modifier preferences
csharp_preferred_modifier_order = public,private,protected,inter-
nal,static,extern,new,virtual,abstract,sealed,override,readon-
ly,unsafe,volatile,async:suggestion
# Expression-level preferences
csharp_prefer_braces = true:silent
csharp_style_deconstructed_variable_declaration = true:suggestion
csharp_prefer_simple_default_expression = true:suggestion
csharp_style_pattern_local_over_anonymous_function = true:sugges-
tion
csharp_style_inlined_variable_declaration = true:suggestion
###############################
# C# Formatting Rules          #
###############################
# New line preferences
csharp_new_line_before_open_brace = all
csharp_new_line_before_else = true
csharp_new_line_before_catch = true
csharp_new_line_before_finally = true
csharp_new_line_before_members_in_object_initializers = true
```

```
csharp_new_line_before_members_in_anonymous_types = true

csharp_new_line_between_query_expression_clauses = true

# Indentation preferences

csharp_indent_case_contents = true

csharp_indent_switch_labels = true

csharp_indent_labels = flush_left

# Space preferences

csharp_space_after_cast = false

csharp_space_after_keywords_in_control_flow_statements = true

csharp_space_between_method_call_parameter_list_parentheses =
false

csharp_space_between_method_declaration_parameter_list_parenthe-
ses = false

csharp_space_between_parentheses = false

csharp_space_before_colon_in_inheritance_clause = true

csharp_space_after_colon_in_inheritance_clause = true

csharp_space_around_binary_operators = before_and_after

csharp_space_between_method_declaration_empty_parameter_list_pa-
rentheses = false

csharp_space_between_method_call_name_and_opening_parenthesis =
false

csharp_space_between_method_call_empty_parameter_list_parentheses
= false

# Wrapping preferences

csharp_preserve_single_line_statements = true

csharp_preserve_single_line_blocks = true

################################

# VB Coding Conventions      #

################################

[*.vb]

# Modifier preferences

visual_basic_preferred_modifier_order = Partial,Default,Pri-
vate,Protected,Public,Friend,NotOverridable,Overridable,MustOver-
ride,Overloads,Overrides,MustInherit,NotInheritable,Static,Sha-
red,Shadows,ReadOnly,WriteOnly,Dim,Const,WithEvents,Widening,Nar-
rowing,Custom,Async:suggestion
```

To open the file again, follow these steps:

1. Save the file. Now it's a part of the solution.

2. Double click the file to open it. This is shown in *Figure 5.10*:

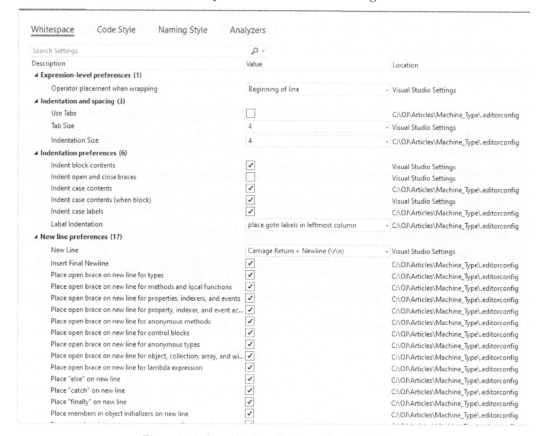

Figure 5.10: *Opened Editor Configuration File Settings*

3. Open **EditorConfig** file.

Conclusion

In this chapter, we explored AI IntelliCode and what it can do for developers. It not only helps finish code lines and signatures but also learns as the teams types their code. IntelliCode also helps in learning about EditorConfig files.

The next chapter (*Built-in Tools*) puts our focus on Tools in Visual Studio 2022. We will explore the new Live Preview, Web Live Preview and have a look at Hot Reload and Force Run.

Key Topics

- IntelliSense

- IntelliCode

- Artificial Intelligence

- Team Completions

- .editorconfig file

Points to remember

- IntelliCode saves us time by putting what we're most likely to use at that point in time at the top of the completion list, thanks to its built-in Artificial Intelligence following recommendations on common practices used by thousands of developers in thousands of open-source projects.

- Visual Studio IntelliCode acts as an extra pair of eyes on our code reviews.

- IntelliCode provides recommendations based on the currently entered code and seamlessly share these recommendations across the development team.

Questions

1. What is the use of an EditorConfig file?

2. Explein the term Artificial Intelligence.

Answers

1. EditorConfig helps us to maintain a consistent coding style while working with multiple developers on the same project with different editors and IDEs.

2. **Artificial Intelligence (AI)**, or Machine Intelligence is simply put: intelligence demonstrated by machines. This means that we can teach machines to do certain tasks, or we can program the so that they are able to learn things themselves.

CHAPTER 6
Built-in Coding Experience Tools

An IDE's real power is its containing tools. Without decent tools, application performance will suffer, creation of the project will take longer and debugging the projects will be limited.

This chapter explores some of the built-in tools Visual Studio 2022 provides to improve our coding experience. We will learn about the various preview tools and have a look at the Force Run and Hot Reload tools. We will also understand the themes and icons provided in Visual Studio 2022.

Structure

In this chapter we will cover the following topics:

- Built-in tools
  - o Hot Reload
  - o Force Run
  - o Updated Icons
  - o Cascadia Code
  - o Product Themes

Objectives

After reading this chapter the developer will have hands-on experience in working with some of the various built-in tools that Visual Studio 2022 provides.

Built-In tools

Any decent IDE is nothing without its tools. Whether the tools are built-in or added on, they improve the hosting **Integrated Development Environment** (**IDE**). In Visual Studio 2022 there are numerous tools to improve your coding experience. Let's have a look at some of them.

Hot Reload

Hot Reload everywhere, for Blazor, ASP.NET Core, .NET Multi-platform App UI (.NET MAUI), Xamarin.Forms, and Winforms allows code changes while running an application, be reflected immediately.

To see Hot Reload in action, let's do a small example:

1. Open Visual Studio 2022.

2. Create a Visual basic Windows Forms application.

3. Edit the form's code to look like the following code segment:

```
Imports System.Math
Public Class Form1

    Private Const intLeaves As Integer = 18
    Private arrColors(intLeaves - 1) As Color

    Private Sub Form1_Paint(ByVal sender As Object, ByVal e As
System.Windows.Forms.PaintEventArgs) Handles MyBase.Paint

        Const dbMinHeight As Double = -11
        Const dbMaxHeight As Double = 11

        Const dbTotalHeight As Double = dbMaxHeight - dbMinHeight

        Dim dbTotalWidth As Double = dbTotalHeight *
Me.ClientSize.Width / Me.ClientSize.Height

        Dim dbMiddle As Double = Me.ClientSize.Height /
dbTotalHeight
```

```vb
        e.Graphics.ScaleTransform(dbMiddle, dbMiddle)
        e.Graphics.TranslateTransform(dbTotalWidth / 2,
-dbMinHeight)

        Const PI As Double = 3.14159265
        Const lngLines As Long = 7500

        Dim i As Long
        Dim a
        Dim b As Double
        Dim ptOne As PointF
        Dim ptTwo As PointF

        a = 0
        ptTwo = New PointF(b * Sin(a), -b * Cos(a))

        Dim pPen As New Pen(Color.Blue, 0)

        For i = 0 To lngLines
            a = i * intLeaves * PI / lngLines

            b = 10 * (1 + Sin(11 * a / 5)) - 4 * Sin(30 * a / 3)
^ 4 * Sin(2 * Cos(3 * a) - 14 * a) ^ 12
            ptOne = ptTwo

            ptTwo = New PointF(b * Sin(a), -b * Cos(a))

            pPen.Color = GetNewColour(a)

            e.Graphics.DrawLine(pPen, ptOne, ptTwo)

        Next i

        pPen.Dispose()

    End Sub

    Private Function GetNewColour(c As Double) As Color

        Return arrColors(Int(c / PI))

    End Function

    Private Sub Form1_Load(ByVal sender As System.Object, ByVal e
```

```
As System.EventArgs) Handles MyBase.Load

        Me.SetStyle(
            ControlStyles.AllPaintingInWmPaint Or
            ControlStyles.DoubleBuffer Or
            ControlStyles.ResizeRedraw,
            True)

        Me.UpdateStyles()

        Me.BackColor = Color.Black

        arrColors = New Color() {
        Color.DarkMagenta,
        Color.Brown,
        Color.Orange,
        Color.SeaShell,
        Color.Beige,
        Color.Aquamarine,
        Color.DodgerBlue,
        Color.Purple,
        Color.Fuchsia,
        Color.Red,
        Color.Chocolate,
        Color.White,
        Color.DarkGreen,
        Color.Gold,
        Color.Blue,
        Color.Violet,
        Color.Pink,
        Color.MistyRose,
        Color.Orange,
        Color.Yellow,
        Color.Chartreuse,
        Color.Teal,
        Color.SkyBlue,
        Color.MediumOrchid
        }
```

```
    End Sub
End Class
```

4. Running the program will produce the following screen:

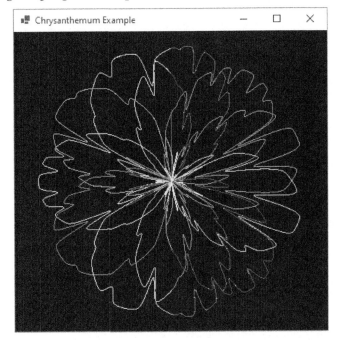

Figure 6.1: *Program run normally*

5. Now, set a break point on the following line: IF NOT KNOW HOW REFER TO

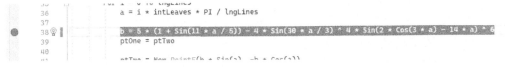

Figure 6.2: *Set a Breakpoint*

6. Run the application. The debugger will stop at the break point.

7. Edit the line to resemble the next picture below. Note the yellow encircled numbers that needs to be replaced/inserted:

Figure 6.3: *Changes to make in code*

8.   Click on the red flame next to **Continue** and select Hot Reload on File Save:

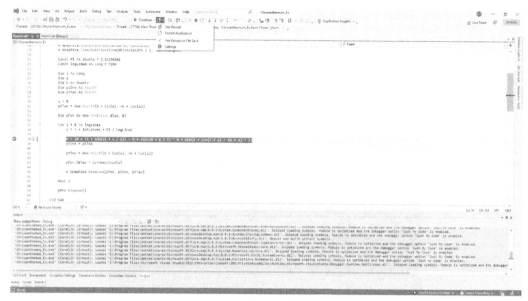

Figure 6.4: *Hot Reload*

9.   Save your changes.

10. Remove the break point.

11. Click **Continue**.

The changes will be reflected, as shown below:

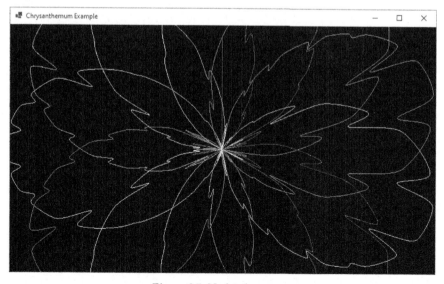

Figure 6.5: *Updated program*

Force Run to Cursor

Setting and removing breakpoints while debugging can be a painful experience. It becomes tedious when a developer has to remove or disable a breakpoint at a certain location, when they have to only test a certain part of code. It becomes more time-consuming when the developer has to continuously Step-over or Step-into code to see what is going on in their code.

Luckily in Visual Studio 2022, Microsoft brought in a feature called Force Run to Cursor. This functionality is quite similar to the already existing Run to Cursor feature. For more information regarding Run to Cursor, please have a look at the *References* section at the end of this chapter. With the Force Run to Cursor feature developers can keep their breakpoints in place while the debugger skips over them, as well as any first chance exceptions break conditions, until the debugger reaches the line of code with the cursor. For more information on First Chance exceptions and First chance exception break conditions, refer to the *References* section at the end of this chapter.

After the cursor has been executed, the breakpoints and first chance exception break conditions go back to their original state.

There is no need to install an extension or tool, or to enable this functionality as it already forms part of the Visual Studio 2022 Debugger. There are two ways to set it in action:

1. Right click on a line and select **Force Run to Cursor**. Refer to the screenshot below for the same:

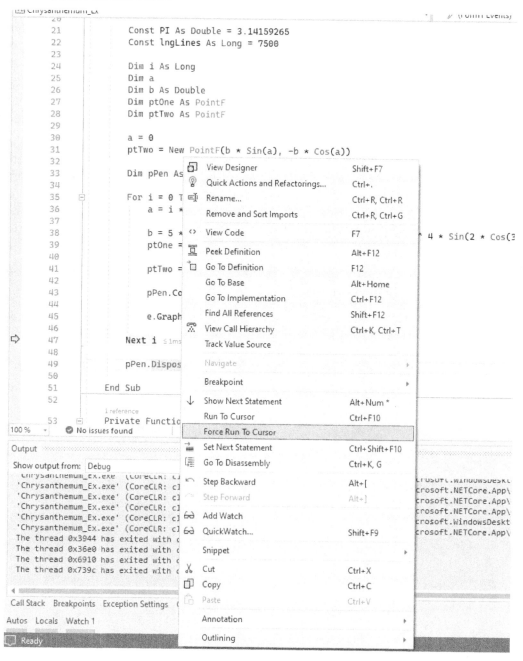

***Figure 6.6**: Right click to Force Run to Cursor*

2. In an active Debug session, press *Shift*, and select **Force run to Cursor** as shown in *figure 6.7*:

```
20
21          Const PI As Double = 3.14159265
22          Const lngLines As Long = 7500
23
24          Dim i As Long
25          Dim a
26          Dim b As Double
27          Dim ptOne As PointF
28          Dim ptTwo As PointF
29
30          a = 0
31          ptTwo = New PointF(b * Sin(a), -b * Cos(a))
32
33          Dim pPen As New Pen(Color.Blue, 0)
34
35     ⊟    For i = 0 To lngLines
36              a = i * intLeaves * PI / lngLines
37
38              b = 5 * (1 + Sin(11 * a / 5)) - 4 * Sin(3
39              ptOne = ptTwo
40
41              ptTwo = New PointF(b * Sin(a), -b * Cos(a
42
43              pPen.Color = GetNewColour(a)
44
45              e.Graphics.DrawLine(pPen, ptOne, ptTwo)
46
47     ▶▶▏ Next i  ≤ 1ms elapsed
48
49          Force run execution to here
```

Figure 6.7: *Force Run to Cursor in Active Debug Session*

Updated Icons

Visual Studio 2022 has updated its icons quite subtly. By the first look, there doesn't seem to be much difference, but by looking closely, Visual Studio 2022 has a more polished and softer look, especially on the eyes. Below is a comparison from the View menu of Visual Studio 2019 and Visual Studio 2022:

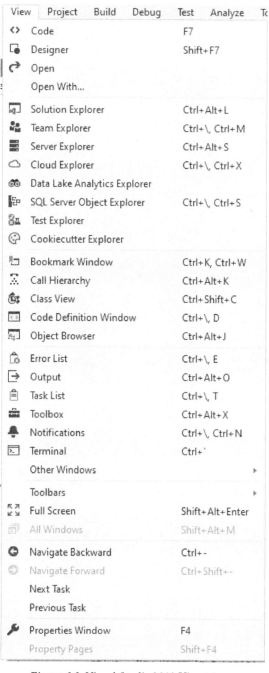

***Figure 6.8**: Visual Studio 2019 View Menu*

The Visual Studio 2022 view menu looks like the following screenshot:

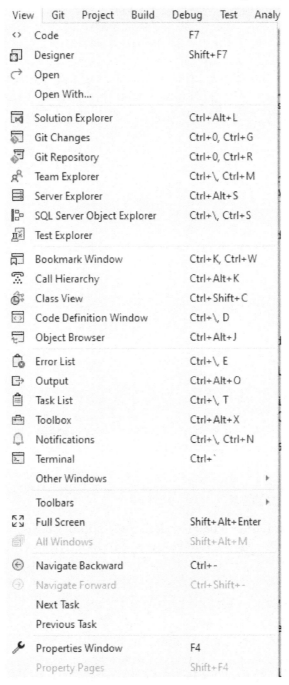

Figure 6.9: Visual Studio 2022 View Menu

Cascadia Code

With Visual Studio 2022 comes the Cascadia Code and Cascadia Mono fonts. The last of which is the default font for Visual Studio 2022. Cascadia is a new, modern, monospaced font family that provides better flexibility for command-line applications and text editor experiences, according to Microsoft. To compare, here are both Visual Studio 2019 (left) and Visual Studio 2022 (right) IDEs displaying the same code in their respective default fonts. Please take a look at the following screenshot:

Figure 6.10: VS 2019 and VS 2022 Code display comparison

Product Themes

Speaking of User Interface changes, let's talk about Product themes. A Product Theme is a theme when set, changes the entire look and feel of the IDE. This is a concept started by Microsoft in Visual Studio Code. For more information on Themes in Visual Studio Code, refer to my book: *Building Cross-Platform Modern Apps using Visual Studio Code (VS Code)*, the link of which is supplied in the *References* section at the end of this chapter.

There are quite a few nice themes that can be set in Visual Studio. Some themes have been converted using the Theme Converter tool. For more information on the Theme Converter tool, have a look at the *References* section at the end of this chapter.

Two nice light themes includes:

- Plural Light theme

- Visual Studio 25th Anniversary Theme pack

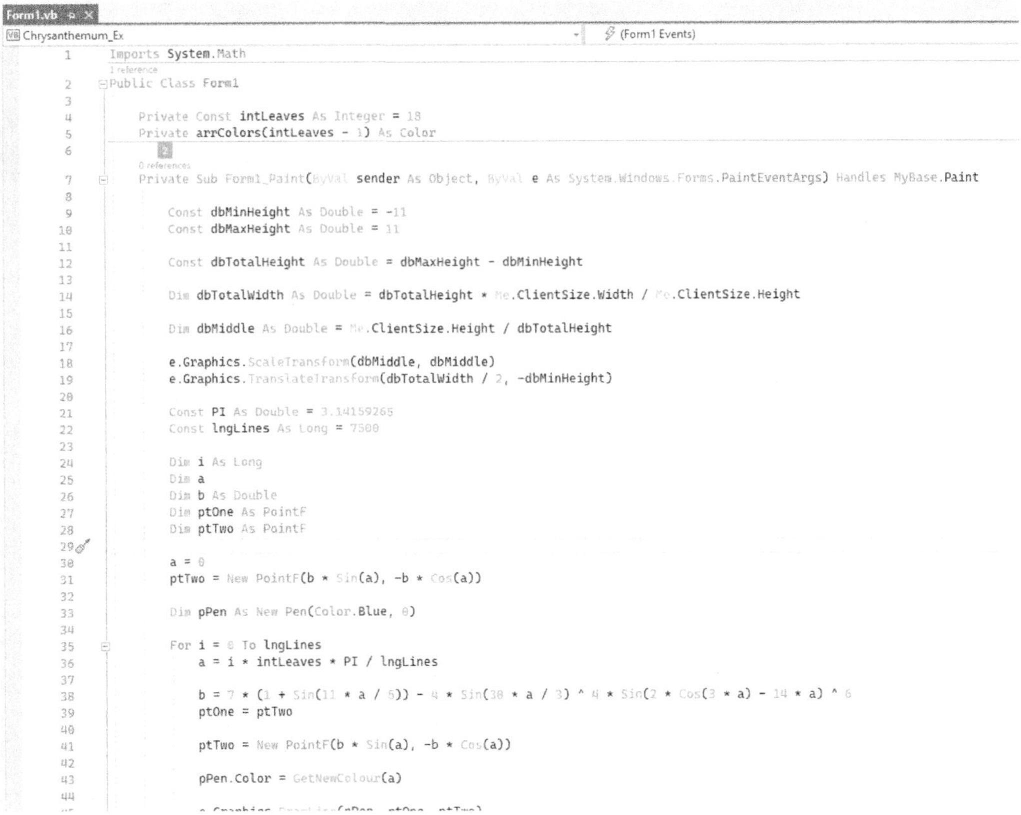

Figure 6.11: *Plural Light Theme*

Setting a theme in Visual Studio 2022

To set a theme in Visual studio 202, follow these steps:

1. Navigate to:

   **https://marketplace.visualstudio.com/
   search?term=theme&target=VS&category=All%20
   categories&vsVersion=vs2022&sortBy=Relevance**

The themes can be seen in *Figure 6.12*:

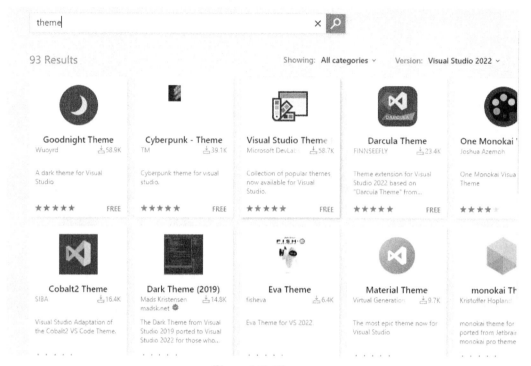

Figure 6.12: Themes

2. Select a theme of your choice.

3. On the page that opens click **Download**. This will download a vsix file (which is a Visual Studio Extension file) as seen in the following screenshot:

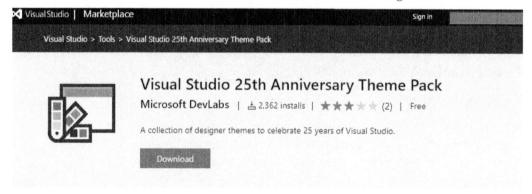

Figure 6.13: Theme to download

4. Open it by double clicking on it – Make sure Visual Studio 2022 is closed, before installing a theme. The page opens as *Figure 6.14*:

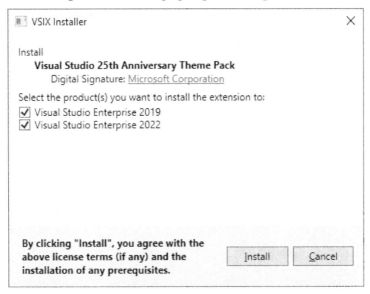

Figure 6.14: *Ready to install*

5. Follow the steps until the theme has been installed:

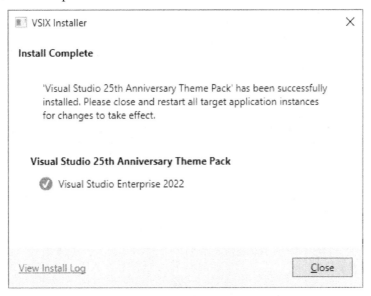

Figure 6.15: *Installation Complete*

6. Open Visual Studio 2022.

7. Navigate to **Tools**.

8. Expand **Theme**.

9. Select the theme.

Figure 6.16: Applying the Theme

Conclusion

This chapter walked us through some of the tools that Visual Studio 2022 provides in order to have a better coding experience.

In the next chapter, *Diagnostics and Debugging,* we will explore the debugging tools in Visual Studio 2022 and how to use them.

Key topics

- Hot Reload
- Force Run

Points to remember

- Hot Reload everywhere, for Blazor, ASP.NET Core, .NET Multi-platform App UI (.NET MAUI), Xamarin.Forms, and Winforms allows code changes while running an application to be reflected immediately.
- With Visual Studio 2022 comes the Cascadia Code and Cascadia Mono fonts.

Questions

1. What is a Product Theme?
2. Define the term: Force Run.

Answers

1. A Product Theme is a theme that can be set that changes the entire look and feel of the IDE.
2. With the Force Run to Cursor feature developers can keep their breakpoints in place while the debugger skips over them, as well as any first chance exceptions break conditions, until the debugger reaches the line of code with the cursor.

References

- **Run to Cursor: https://devblogs.microsoft.com/visualstudio/debug-with-force-run-to-cursor/#:~:text=Starting%20with%20Visual%20Studio%20 2022,of%20code%20with%20the%20cursor.**
- **First chance exceptions: https://docs.microsoft.com/en-us/visualstudio/ debugger/managing-exceptions-with-the-debugger?view=vs-2022**
- **Web Live Preview: https://docs.microsoft.com/en-us/shows/visual-studio-toolbox/web-live-preview**
- **Accessibility Insights: https://devblogs.microsoft.com/visualstudio/lets-make-visual-studio-even-more-accessible-together/**

- **Building Cross-Platform Modern Apps using Visual Studio Code (VS Code):** https://www.amazon.com/gp/product/B09VL3T6GX/ref=dbs_a_def_rwt_bibl_vppi_i2

- **Theme Converter Tool:** https://github.com/microsoft/theme-converter-for-vs

CHAPTER 7
Diagnostics and Debugging Tools

The term *"bug"* has an interesting origin. At 3:45 PM on September 9, 1947, *Grace Murray Hopper* records the first instance of a bug being found, in the Harvard Mark II computer's logbook. The actual bug was a moth that got stuck between relay contacts in the computer, hence the term *"bug"*.

A bug in software, is any error, flaw, failure, or fault in a computer program that causes the program to behave unintendedly or produce a wrong or unexpected result. Debugging is the process of finding and fixing bugs in a computer program. Interestingly, the term *"debugging"* was used (in 1945 in airplane engine testing) even before the first computer bug was found in 1947. Only in 1950, software developers started using the term *"bug"*.

To debug, we need debugging tools.

In this chapter we will learn about the awesome debugging tools Visual Studio 2022 has as well as their innerworkings.

Structure

In this chapter we will discuss the following topics:

- Code clean-up
- Search bar on debugging windows

- Debugging in general

- Visual Studio 2022 remote debugging tools

- Instrumentation profiler

- T-SQL debugger

Objectives

This chapter focuses on the tools to help fixing program errors locally and remotely. It explores the next search features in the debugging windows to find values of objects quicker. The chapter also focuses on tools to help code better and faster.

Code cleanup

In *Chapter 1, Getting Started with Visual Studio 2022*, we briefly discussed the Document Health Indicator. The Document Health Indicator enables us to check and maintain our code's issues. It works because of its Code Cleanup command. With Code Cleanup we can identify and fix warnings and suggestions with one simple click of a button.

Code Cleanup formats the code and applies all code fixes as suggested by its current settings and `.editorconfig` files. EditorConfig files, as discussed in depth in *Chapter 3, C# 9 Language & Coding Changes*, helps us maintain a consistent coding style while working with multiple developers on the same project with different editors and IDEs. An EditorConfig project consists of a file format that defines coding styles, and plugins that enable editors to read the file format and adhere to defined styles.

The Health Inspector can be accessed at the bottom of the Code Window, indicated by a little brush icon. The Code Window can be accessed by any of the following methods:

- Pressing *F7* anywhere in the Design Window

- Right clicking anywhere in the Design Window, and selecting **View Code**

- Right clicking on the file in the Solution Explorer, and selecting **View Code**

The Document Health Inspector is shown in the following screenshot:

Figure 7.1: Document Health Indicator

There are two built-in profiles:

One is pre-set but can be edited. Profile 2 is initially empty but can be set and amended at any time. To edit these profiles, we need to Configure the Code Cleanup.

The fixers available for the profiles might seem familiar to experienced Visual Studio users, as they are modelled after the Text Formatting options that was found under the following menu:

- Tools
- Options
- Text Editor
- C#

Figure 7.2 shows the configuration screen once **Configure Code Cleanup** has been selected from the menu:

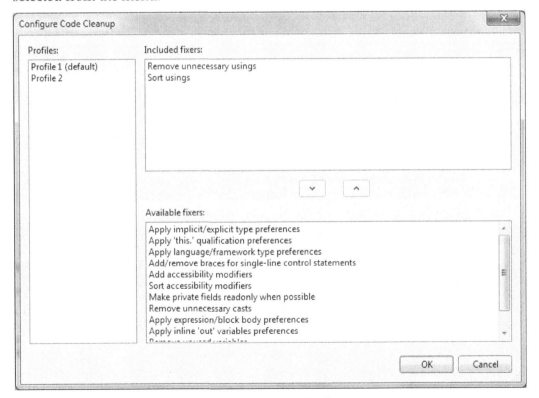

Figure 7.2: *Configure Code Cleanup*

Figure 7.3 shows the code formatting and refactoring options available in the C#
Code formatting **Options** screen.

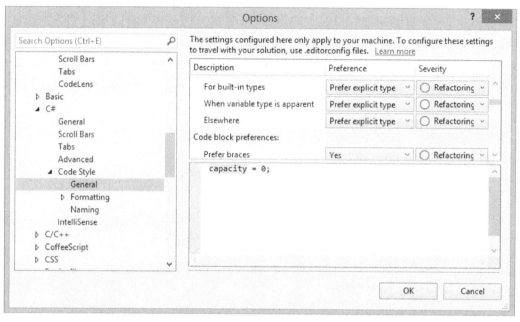

Figure 7.3: *Code Formatting options*

Profile 1 includes two fixers:

- Remove unnecessary usings

  Remove unnecessary usings removes the usings that C# includes in code
  files by default. How does it know what is necessary and what is not?
  Well, when looking at a C# code file, the usings are at the top of the file.
  The namespaces included provides the functionality to make use of code
  that might not ordinarily exist in the code file. For example: When dealing
  with heavy math-oriented methods, the **System.Math** namespace should be
  included.

  By looking at the included namespaces, there might be faded lines in
  between, as shown next. These usings are unnecessary and can be removed:

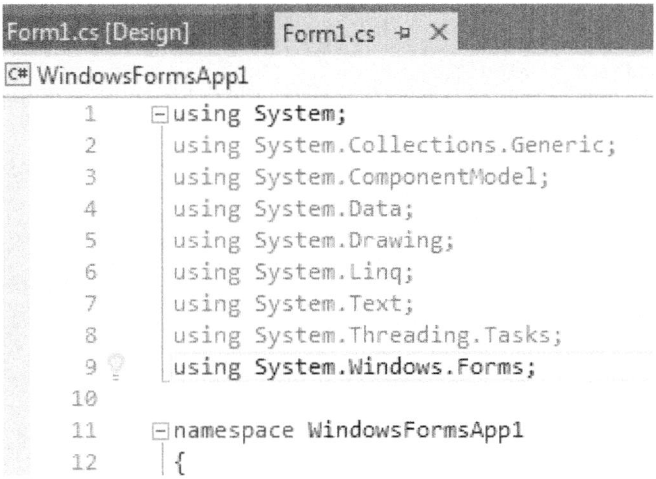

Figure 7.4: *Unnecessary usings*

- Sort usings

  Sort usings improves readability of the included namespaces and organizes them nicely.

  By running Profile 1, it will remove and sort usings.

Let's have a look at the other fixers available, and what we can do with them.

Applying implicit / explicit type preferences

The Apply implicit / explicit type preferences fixer converts every **var** variable to explicit types, or the other way around. The var keyword in C# can be used instead of a type when declaring variables. This causes the compiler to simply infer the type of the variable.

A local variable implicitly typed with **var**, is strongly typed, but the compiler still determines its type. The following two declarations are functionally equivalent:

```
var Age = 40; // Implicitly typed.
int Age = 40; // Explicitly typed.
```

Applying 'this.' qualification preferences

The **this** C# keyword appertains to the current instance of a class. The **this.** keyword has the following uses:

- Qualify members hidden by similar names

```
public class Student
{
    private string FirstName;
    private string LastName;
    public Student(string FirstName, string LastName)
    {
        // Use this to qualify the members of the class
        this.FirstName = FirstName;
        this.LastName = LastName;
    }
}
```

- Pass an object as a parameter to methods

```
GetMarks(this);
```

- Declare indexers

```
public int this[int param]
{
    get { return array[param]; }
    set { array[param] = value; }
}
```

The Apply 'this.' qualification preferences fixer applies 'this.' preferences where it deems necessary.

Applying language/framework type preferences

The Apply language/framework type preferences fixer converts framework types to language types, or vice versa.

Add/remove braces for single-line control statements

The Add/remove braces for single-line control statements fixer adds or removes curly braces from single-line control statements such as if and for. In the example below, both if statements are similar:

```
if(condition)
{
        //Statement
}

if(condition)
        //Statement
```

Add accessibility modifiers

Access modifiers enables us to declare an object with certain accessibility. In C# there are four access modifiers:

- public
- protected
- internal
- private

Although there are four access modifiers, there are six accessibility levels that can be specified:

Access Modifier	Accessibility Level
Public	No restrictions
Protected	Containing class or derived types from containing class
Internal	Current assembly
protected internal	Current assembly or derived types from containing class
Private	Containing type or class
private protected	Containing class or derived types from containing class in current assembly

Table 7.1: Accessibility Levels

The Add accessibility modifiers fixer adds missing accessibility modifiers where necessary.

Sort accessibility modifiers

The Sort accessibility modifiers fixer sorts accessibility modifiers nicely.

Make private fields read-only when possible

When fields are private and read-only we can't change the value unintentionally from another part of a class after the field's initialization. Private read-only fields can only be changed in the Class' constructor, or by the field's initialization. The Make private fields read-only, when possible, fixer makes private fields read-only wherever possible.

Remove unnecessary casts

Casting is a method of converting values from one type to another. There are two types of casts:

- Implicit casting

  The compilers cast the values automatically if no loss of information occurs. Usually, this cast involves converting a smaller data type to a larger data type.

  ```
  int SmallNumber = 2147483647; //2147483647 = Max positive value
  for 32-bit signed integer

  long BigNumber = SmallNumber; //long accepts the value because it
  has a larger range
  ```

- Explicit casting

  The developer specifies the type of casting, with the risk of possibly losing data.

  ```
  float DecimalNumber = 1523647.87; //Specify floating point number

  int WholeNumber;

  WholeNumber = (int)DecimalNumber; //Cast Decimal to Integer
  resulting in: 1523647.
  ```

  The Remove unnecessary casts fixer removes unnecessary casts where possible

Apply expression/block body preferences

The Apply expression/block body preferences fixer converts expression-bodied members to block bodies or block bodies to expression-bodied members.

Apply inline 'out' variables preferences

In earlier versions of C#, to use an out variable, it must first have been declared a variable of the correct type, then use it typically on the next line of code as an out parameter, for example:

```
DateTime StartTime;
if (DateTime.TryParse(DateTime.Now.ToShortDateString(), out StartTime))
{
    // Use StartTime.
}
```

The Apply inline 'out' variables preferences fixe inline out variables wherever possible. The previous code segment can now look like:

```
if (DateTime.TryParse(DateTime.Now.ToShortDateString(), out DateTime
StartTime))
{
    // Use StartTime.
}
```

Remove unused variables

The Remove unused variables fixer removes all variables that haven't been used.

Apply object/collection initialization preferences

Object or Collection initializers enables us to assign values to fields or properties of an object upon creation, without invoking a constructor and lines of assignments. For example:

```
Student student = new Student { Age = 40, Name = "Ockert" };
```

The Apply object/collection initialization preferences fixer uses object and collection initializers wherever possible.

Search bar on debugging windows

The Watch, Autos, and Locals windows includes a new search feature that enables us to find your variables and their properties faster. With this new search feature, we can highlight and navigate to specified values which are contained within the name, value, and type columns of the watch window.

Search and highlighting

When entering text in the search bar, the highlighting of matches which are currently expanded on the screen will occur, this gives us a faster option to perform a large-scale search. This is shown in the following screenshot:

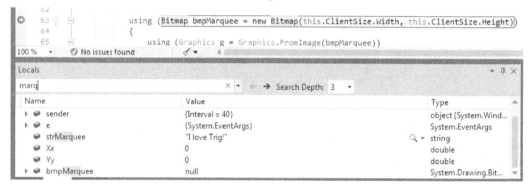

Figure 7.5: Search and Highlighting

Search navigation

To commence searching in any of the Watch windows, enter the query and press *Enter*, or, even easier, press the left (Find Next, or *F3*) and right (Find Previous, or *Shift + F3*) arrows. These search icons also navigate through each found match. Please take a look at the following screenshot:

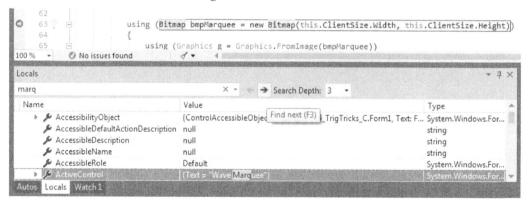

Figure 7.6: Search Navigation

Search depth

The debugging watch windows provide a Search Depth drop down to find matches nested deep into your objects, giving us the power to choose how thorough the search should be. It can be seen in *Figure 7.7*:

Figure 7.7: Search Depth

Debugging applications – Debugging in general

When debugging applications in Visual Studio 2022, the application that is being debugged is running with the Visual Studio debugger attached. The debugger provides many ways and tools to see what the application's code is doing while it runs. This includes:

- Stepping through the code to look at the values stored in objects
- Watches on variables can be set to determine when values change
- Examine the execution path of the application's code

Breakpoints

Setting a breakpoint indicates Visual Studio where it should suspend the application's running code so that variables' values can be inspected, the behaviour of memory can be determined, and whether a certain piece of code is getting run is checked.

To set a breakpoint follow these steps:

1. Click with the mouse on the left margin. A Maroon dot should appear. This is the Breakpoint.

2. Start the Program, by clicking **Start**.

A Breakpoint is shown as follows:

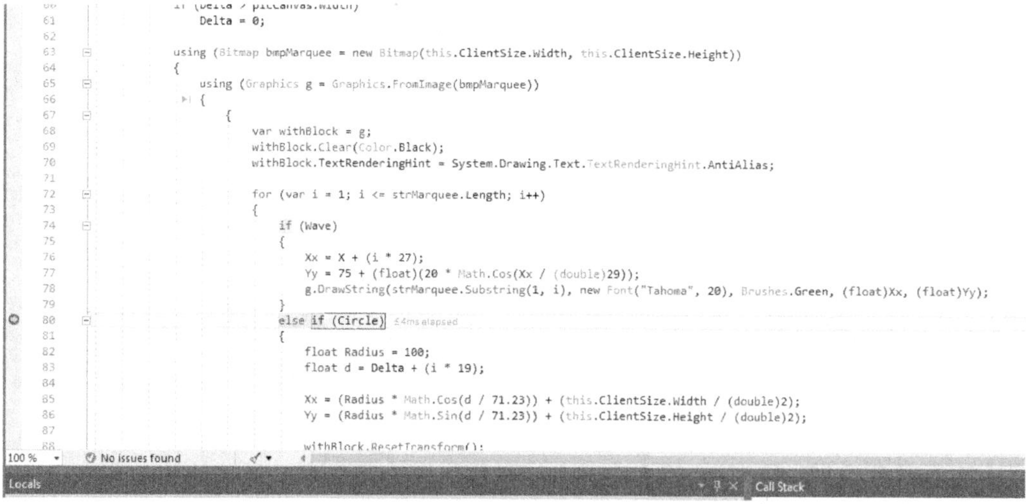

```
60          if (Delta > picCanvas.Width)
61              Delta = 0;
62
63          using (Bitmap bmpMarquee = new Bitmap(this.ClientSize.Width, this.ClientSize.Height))
64          {
65              using (Graphics g = Graphics.FromImage(bmpMarquee))
66              {
67                  {
68                      var withBlock = g;
69                      withBlock.Clear(Color.Black);
70                      withBlock.TextRenderingHint = System.Drawing.Text.TextRenderingHint.AntiAlias;
71
72                      for (var i = 1; i <= strMarquee.Length; i++)
73                      {
74                          if (Wave)
75                          {
76                              Xx = X + (i * 27);
77                              Yy = 75 + (float)(20 * Math.Cos(Xx / (double)29));
78                              g.DrawString(strMarquee.Substring(1, i), new Font("Tahoma", 20), Brushes.Green, (float)Xx, (float)Yy);
79                          }
80                          else if (Circle)   84ms elapsed
81                          {
82                              float Radius = 100;
83                              float d = Delta + (i * 19);
84
85                              Xx = (Radius * Math.Cos(d / 71.23)) + (this.ClientSize.Width / (double)2);
86                              Yy = (Radius * Math.Sin(d / 71.23)) + (this.ClientSize.Height / (double)2);
87
88                              withBlock.ResetTransform();
```
```
100 %  ▼   ⊘ No issues found            ✓ ▼  ◄
Locals                                              ▼ ₽ × | Call Stack
```

Figure 7.8: Breakpoint

Navigating code during debug mode

We navigate running code with the use of stepping commands:

- Step Into (F11)

  The debugger steps through code statements one at a time as shown in *figure 7.9*:

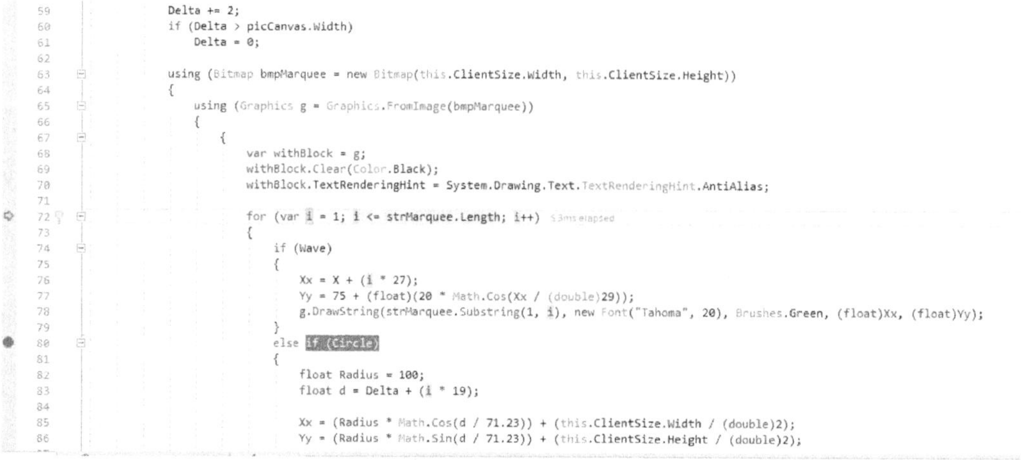

```
59          Delta += 2;
60          if (Delta > picCanvas.Width)
61              Delta = 0;
62
63          using (Bitmap bmpMarquee = new Bitmap(this.ClientSize.Width, this.ClientSize.Height))
64          {
65              using (Graphics g = Graphics.FromImage(bmpMarquee))
66              {
67                  {
68                      var withBlock = g;
69                      withBlock.Clear(Color.Black);
70                      withBlock.TextRenderingHint = System.Drawing.Text.TextRenderingHint.AntiAlias;
71
72                      for (var i = 1; i <= strMarquee.Length; i++)   53ms elapsed
73                      {
74                          if (Wave)
75                          {
76                              Xx = X + (i * 27);
77                              Yy = 75 + (float)(20 * Math.Cos(Xx / (double)29));
78                              g.DrawString(strMarquee.Substring(1, i), new Font("Tahoma", 20), Brushes.Green, (float)Xx, (float)Yy);
79                          }
80                          else if (Circle)
81                          {
82                              float Radius = 100;
83                              float d = Delta + (i * 19);
84
85                              Xx = (Radius * Math.Cos(d / 71.23)) + (this.ClientSize.Width / (double)2);
86                              Yy = (Radius * Math.Sin(d / 71.23)) + (this.ClientSize.Height / (double)2);
```

Figure 7.9: Step Into

- Step Over (F10)

Step Over steps over the execution of functions. This mean that it will execute the function without pauses, and only pause on the next statement after the function.

```
62
63      using (Bitmap bmpMarquee = new Bitmap(this.ClientSize.Width, this.ClientSize.Height))
64      {
65          using (Graphics g = Graphics.FromImage(bmpMarquee))
66          {
67              {
68                  var withBlock = g;
69                  withBlock.Clear(Color.Black);
70                  withBlock.TextRenderingHint = System.Drawing.Text.TextRenderingHint.AntiAlias;
71
72                  for (var i = 1; i <= strMarquee.Length; i++)
73                  {
74                      if (Wave)  ≤2ms elapsed
75                      {
76                          Xx = X + (i * 27);
77                          Yy = 75 + (float)(20 * Math.Cos(Xx / (double)29));
78                          g.DrawString(strMarquee.Substring(1, i), new Font("Tahoma", 20), Brushes.Green, (float)Xx, (float)Yy);
79                      }
80                      else   (Circle)
81                      {
82                          float Radius = 100;
83                          float d = Delta + (i * 19);
84
85                          Xx = (Radius * Math.Cos(d / 71.23)) + (this.ClientSize.Width / (double)2);
86                          Yy = (Radius * Math.Sin(d / 71.23)) + (this.ClientSize.Height / (double)2);
```

Figure 7.10: Step Over

- Step Out (Shift + F11)

Step Out continues running code and pauses execution when the current function returns.

- Step Into Specific

The Step Into Specific command steps into a specific field or property.

- Run to cursor & Force Run to Cursor

The Run to Cursor and Force Run to Cursor (explained in *Chapter 6, Built-in Tools*) starts debugging and sets a temporary breakpoint on the current line of code where the cursor is.

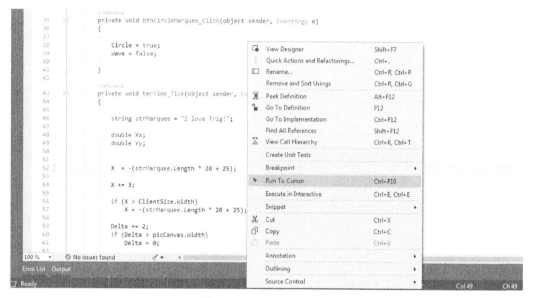

Figure 7.11: Run to Cursor

Debug multiple processes

Visual Studio 2022 can debug a solution that has more than one process. It can switch between processes, break, and step through source, and detach from individual processes.

To debug multiple processes at the same time, use the following steps:

1. Right click the **Solution** in the Solution Explorer.

2. Select **Properties**.

3. On the **Properties** page, select **Common Properties**.

4. Select **Startup Project**.

5. Select **Multiple startup projects**.

6. Select **Start from the Action list**.

7. Click **OK**.

This is illustrated in *Figure 7.12*:

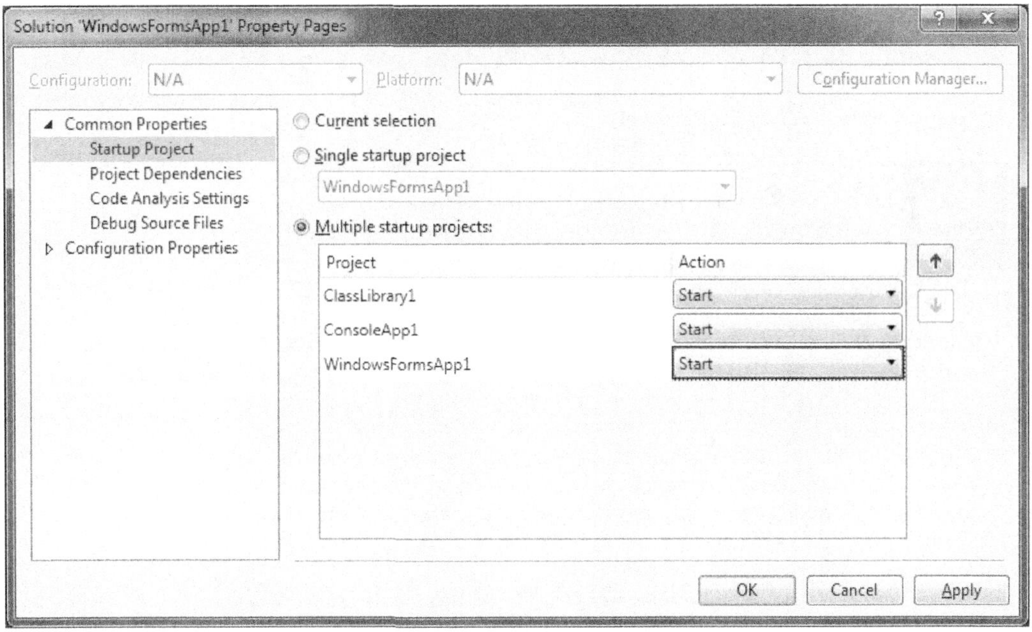

Figure 7.12: Solution Start-up Project Properties

Visual Studio 2022 remote debugging tools

We can debug Visual Studio 2022 applications that were deployed onto a different computer. To do this, we need to use the Visual Studio remote debugging tools. To debug applications that have been deployed onto a different computer, follow these steps:

1. Download the Remote tools.

2. Install and run the remote tools on the computer onto which the application was deployed.

3. Configure the necessary project(s) to connect to the remote computer from Visual Studio.

4. Run the application.

5. Download the Remote Debugging tools.

6. Navigate to the following URL and download the tools according to the desired platform:

   https://visualstudio.microsoft.com/downloads/#remote-tools-for-visual-studio-2022

7. Install and run the Remote Configuration Wizard.

8. After the Remote tools have been downloaded, it needs to be installed and configured. *Figure 7.13* shows the Remote Tools setup screen:

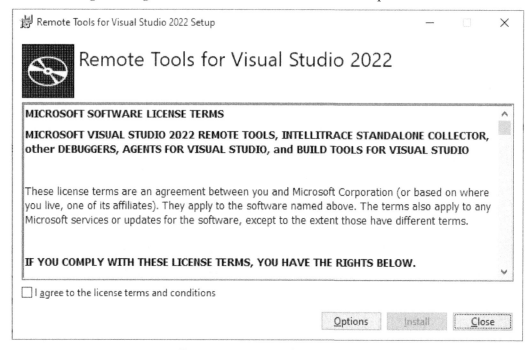

Figure 7.13: *Remote Debugging Tools*

The tools need to be configured. Find the Visual Studio Remote Debugger Configuration Wizard from the Start menu and run it.

The Wizard opens. And a few things need to be set:

- User account and password information

- The following networks for the Firewall

  o Domain networks

  o Private networks

  o Informal or Public networks

- When the Configure remote debugging button is clicked, the Remote debugger window appears

The Remoted Debugger Configuration Wizard screen is displayed in *Figure 7.14*:

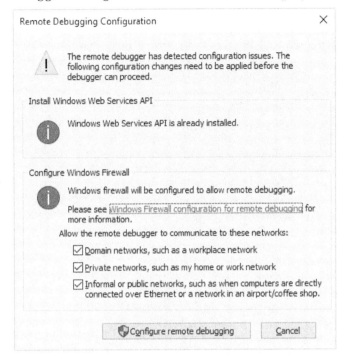

Figure 7.14: *Remote Debugger Configuration Wizard*

Instrumentation profiler

There are two ways of collecting data with profiling:

Collection via instrumentation

Each function call in an application gets annotated and instrumented. Upon invocation the function call is added to the trace along with information about the caller.

Collection via sampling

In sampling, the current call stack is estimated from the CPU at a certain interval and then each frame is added to the trace.

The new dynamic instrumentation tool shows the exact number of times the application's functions are called, it is faster than previous static instrumentation tools and supports .NET Core instrumentation.

To access the new dynamic instrumentation profiling tool, follow these steps:

1. Select **Debug**.

2. Select **Performance Profiler**, as shown below in *Figure 7.15*.

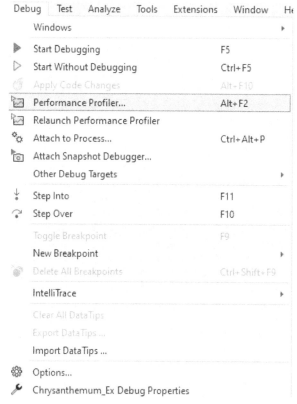

Figure 7.15: Selecting the Performance Profiler

3. Select **Instrumentation**.

4. Click the **Start** button as shown in *Figure 7.16*.

Figure 7.16 : Instrumentation Profiler

Notice that there is a small gear next to Instrumentation. This brings up the following box where settings can be set. For more information on all the settings of the Instrumentation Profiler, please refer to the *References* section at the end of this chapter.

5. Select the specific project, then Click *OK*. Refer to *Figure 7.17*:

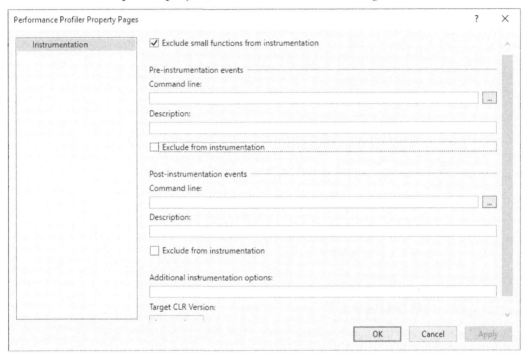

Figure 7.17: *Instrumentation Profiler Settings*

6. The program will be built and run while the profiling is active:

Currently profiling. Pause profiling.

Stop profiling or exit the application to generate a report.

Figure 7.18: *Profiling is active*

When the profiler stops, or the 'Stop Profiling' link (as shown in *Figure 7.18*) is clicked, a detailed report like *Figure 7.19* is shown indicating the CPU usage, the functions doing the most work. It also provides a Hot path where we can navigate through the function calling process.

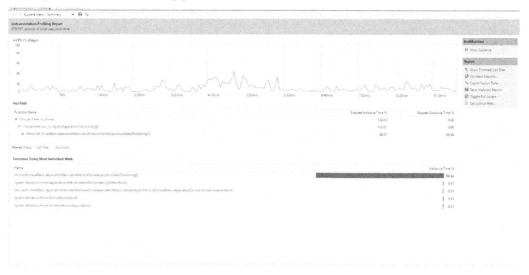

Figure 7.19: *Instrumentation Profiler results*

T-SQL debugger

We can debug SQL Stored Procedures through Visual Studio 2022. This exercise assumes that a database with a stored procedure has been set up.

To do this follow the next few steps:

1. Select **View**.

2. Select **SQL Server Object Explorer** as shown in *Figure 7.20*:

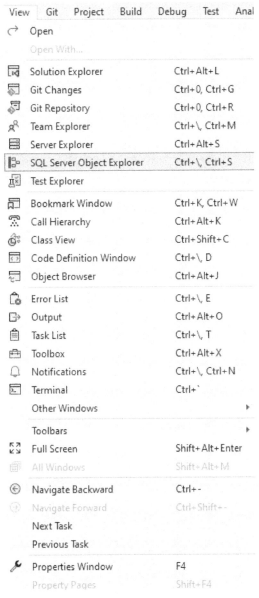

Figure 7.20: *View, SQL Object Explorer*

This will show the SQL Server Object Explorer pane. Some database details have been removed in this following screenshot:

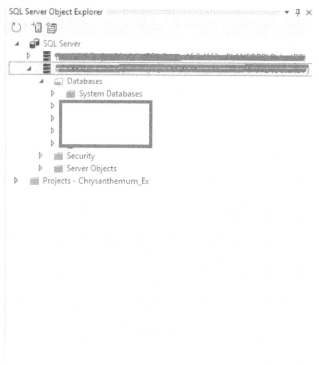

Figure 7.21: SQL Server Object Explorer

3. Expand the Stored Procedures of the chosen database.

4. Right click on a **Stored Procedure**.

5. Select **Debug Procedure** as shown in the following screenshot :

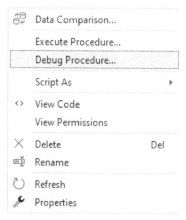

Figure 7.22: Debug Stored Procedure

Conclusion

This chapter gave us some insight into some of the exciting debugging tools that Visual Studio 2022 provides. We learnt how to do profiling to determine how many times functions get called in our applications. We had a look at debugging in general as well as the Visual Studio 2022 remote debugging tools.

In the next chapter (*Digging in the Visual Studio 2022 IDE*), we will explore some of the collaboration tools in Visual Studio 2022.

Key topics

- Search bar
- Debugging
- Instrumentation profiling

Points to remember

- Remove unnecessary usings removes the usings that C# includes in code files by default.
- The Sort accessibility modifiers fixer sorts accessibility modifiers nicely.
- Visual Studio 2022 can debug a solution that has more than one process.
- We can debug SQL Stored Procedures through Visual Studio 2022.

Questions

1. What is the purpose of the Code Cleanup Command in the Document Health Indicator?
2. Which debugging windows allow us to search object values quickly?

Answers

1. With Code Clean-up we can identify and fix warnings and suggestions with one simple click of a button.
2. The Watch, Autos, and Locals windows.

References

Instrumentation profiler settings: https://docs.microsoft.com/en-us/visualstudio/profiling/optimize-profiler-settings?view=vs-2022

Coded UI Test: https://docs.microsoft.com/en-us/visualstudio/test/use-ui-automation-to-test-your-code?view=vs-2022

Section - III
Advanced Tools

Section III covers advanced tools for ASP.NET, mobile devices and Azure Cloud computing. In ASP.NET tools we will learn about the various Web Frameworks at our disposal to create proper Web applications. We will also cover .NET Core 3.1 and talk about third party tools and Extensions.

## CHAPTER 8

Web Tools and Extensions

In this chapter, we will learn about the various Web Frameworks at our disposal to create proper Web applications. We will cover .NET Core 3.1 and talk about third party tools and extensions. These extensions and tools include Blazor which lets browsers interpret C# natively We will also have a look into Web API.

Structure

In this chapter, we will cover the following topics:

- Web Frameworks
- Blazor
- Web API
- Azure

Objectives

This chapter focuses on the tools to enhance our web applications, where to find them, how to install them, and most importantly, how to make use of them.

Web Frameworks

A web framework (or web application framework) is a framework that supports the development of web applications, web services, web resources, and web APIs. They provide a standard way to build and deploy web applications onto the World Wide Web. They also automate the overhead associated with everyday activities by providing libraries for database access, supplying templating frameworks, and providing libraries for session management.

Although numerous web frameworks are available, we will discuss the three most popular ones.

ASP.NET MVC Framework

ASP.NET MVC is a web application framework that implements the **model–view–controller** (**MVC**) pattern. It is a design pattern that decouples the user-interface (view), data (model), and application logic (controller). With the MVC pattern, requests get routed to a Controller (application logic) responsible for working with the model (data) to perform actions or retrieve data. The Controller (application logic) chooses the view to display and then provides the View model (data). The view renders the page based on the data in the model.

The ASP.NET MVC web framework is composed of three roles:

Model (or Business Layer)

Model corresponds to the data-related logic that the user will work with. The model represents the business logic and operations that it should perform. Along with the business logic, implementation logic for persisting data should be encapsulated by the model.

View (or Display Layer)

View represents the User Interface logic of an application. A View's responsibility is to present content via the user interface. It uses the Razor view engine to embed .NET code into HTML markup. Logic within a view should relate to presenting content and be minimal.

Controller (or Input Control)

Controller is an interface between `Model` and `View` components which processes the business logic and interact with the views. Controllers handle user interaction, work with the model, and select views to render. The controller is the entry point and selects which model types to work with and which view to render.

To create an ASP.NET MVC application, follow these steps:

1. Install Visual Studio 2022, as explained in *Chapter 1, Getting to Know the Visual Studio 2022 IDE*, if necessary.

2. Install the ASP.NET and web development workload, as explained in *Chapter 1, Getting to Know the Visual Studio 2022 IDE*, if necessary.

3. Create a new Visual Studio 2022 project.

4. Ensure that ASP.NET Web Application is selected.

   Figure 8.1 shows what it should look like when the ASP.NET Web Application is selected:

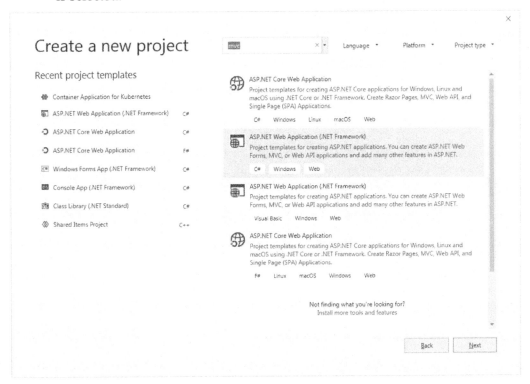

Figure 8.1: ASP.NET MVC Application

5. Click **Next**.

6. Specify the Project details.

7. Click **Create**.

8. Select **MVC**.

9. Select **Create**.

The Solution Explorer includes a Model, Views and Controller folders, and a **HomeController.cs** file, which looks like the following:

```
using System.Web.Mvc;

namespace WebApplication5.Controllers
{
    public class HomeController : Controller
    {
        public ActionResult Index()
        {
            return View();
        }

        public ActionResult About()
        {
            ViewBag.Message = "Your application description page.";

            return View();
        }

        public ActionResult Contact()
        {
            ViewBag.Message = "Your contact page.";

            return View();
        }
    }
}
```

DotNetNuke (DNN Platform)

DNN Platform is a free, open-source content management system. **DotNetNuke (DNN)** makes use of a three-tier architecture model with a core framework that provides support to the extensible modular structure.

The functionality of DotNetNuke can be expanded by adding third-party modules. It can be expanded from an existing module store, 3rd party authors, or in-house development. A DNN skinning architecture provides separation of presentation and content. This enables web designers to develop skins without requiring any development knowledge.

Using DotNetNuke

To get started with the DNN Platform, follow the next few steps:

1. Navigate to the following URL: **https://www.dnnsoftware.com/community/download**

2. Select **Download**.

3. Extract the downloaded zipped files.

4. Create a directory in the **c:\inetpub\wwwroot** folder called DotNetNuke.

5. Copy the contents of the extracted DNN INSTALL package into the **c:\inetpub\wwwroot\dotnetnuke** *folder.*

6. Go to the properties of the **c:\inetpub\wwwroot\dotnetnuke** folder by right clicking it.

7. Click on the **Security** tab.

8. Give this account modify permissions on the folder.

9. Open up the web server IIS Console: start, run, INETMGR

10. Expand websites.

11. Expand default website.

12. Right click on the **dotnetnuke** folder.

13. Click on **Convert to Application**.

14. Browse to the following URL: **http://localhost/dotnetnuke**

15. Step through the installation wizard.

16. The default login accounts should be displayed.

MonoRail

MonoRail is an open-source web application framework. It enforces separation of concerns using a **model–view–controller** (**MVC**) architecture. Ruby on Rails Action Pack inspires it. MonoRail differs from normal ASP.NET Web Forms development by enforcing separation of concerns via the MVC architecture. It maps web requests to an action (a common method on the controller). The controller invokes business services and controls the application's flow. Upon sending web responses to a client, the controller sets a view template to be rendered by putting data in a Property Bag.

To download MonoRail, navigate to the following URL:

https://github.com/castleproject-deprecated/MonoRail

Blazor

Blazor is a web framework that enables us to write client-side web applications using C# via WebAssembly and RAZOR hence, C# can run natively in all four major browsers: Firefox, Chrome, Safari, and Edge. WebAssembly applications get passed to the browser in a binary format that can run natively at near-native speed. A Razor Page is similar to the view component that ASP.NET MVC employs with the same syntax and functionality.

Getting started with Blazor and Visual Studio 2022

In order to get started with Blazor we need the following:

- Visual Studio 19 or higher

- .Net Core SDK 3.1 Preview (or later)

- The Blazor extensions

- Blazor templates

We have Visual Studio 2022, so all we need are the last three items in the list: The .NET Core SDK 3.0 Preview (or later), the Blazor extensions (which we can get from the Visual Studio Market Place) and the Blazor Templates. We will add them now.

> **Note: Chapter 5 covered .NET Core 3.0, and how to download it and it is not much different from installing .NET Core 3.1. If the SDK for .NET Core is already installed, the step pertaining to its download and installation, can be skipped.**

Setting up Blazor

In order to set up Blazor in its entirety, use the following steps:

1. Navigate to: **https://dotnet.microsoft.com/download/dotnet/3.1** to download Core 3.1

   Figure 8.2 displays the .NET Core 3.1 download screen. These options were available at the time of printing of this book. More options may be reflected.

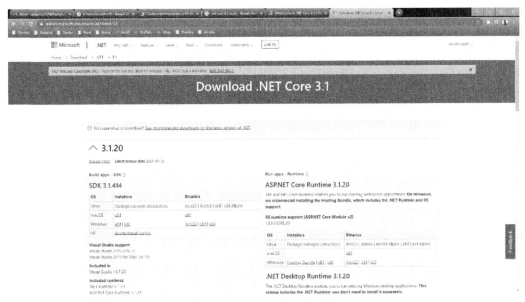

Figure 8.2: .NET Core 3.1 SDK Download

2. After the download, launch the installer. The next screen will be displayed.

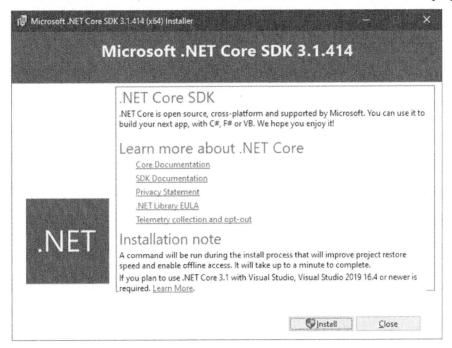

Figure 8.3 : .NET Core 3.1 SDK Installer

3. Install it.

4. Open the developer command prompt and enter the following command: `dotnet new -I Microsoft.AspNetCore.Blazor.Templates::3.0.0-preview5-19227-01`

5. Wait for the confirmation that the Blazor templates have been installed. *Figure 8.4* displays confirmation that the Blazor templates have been installed :

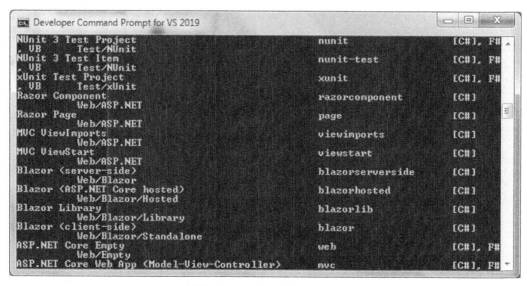

Figure 8.4 : *Blazor templates*

6. To download Blazor, navigate to the following link: **https://marketplace. visualstudio.com/items?itemName=aspnet.blazor**

7. Click **Download** to download the Blazor Extension.

8. Install the VSIX file.

9. Open Visual Studio 2022.

10. Click **Tools**.

11. Options.

12. Select the Projects and Solutions node.

13. Click on **.NET Core**.

14. Check the box for Use previews of the .NET Core SDK, as shown next.

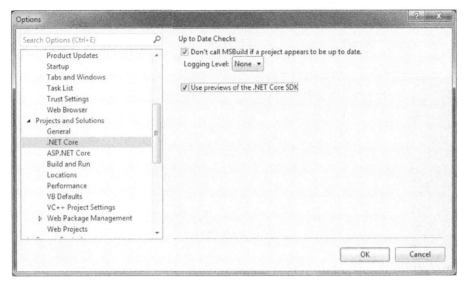

Figure 8.5: SDK Options

15. Click **OK**.

16. Create a new ASP.NET Core Web Application project (if the .NET Core cross-platform development Workload has been installed).

17. Select Blazor (Client-side) as shown here:

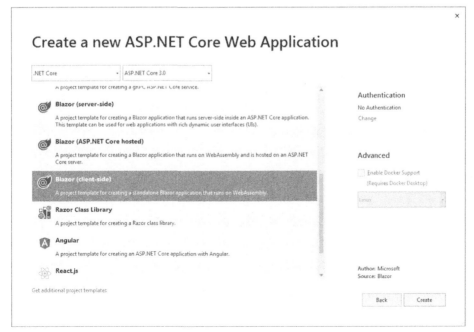

Figure 8.6: Blazor client side

18. Click **Create**.

19. After the project loads, click **Run**. The following screen will appear in the browser.

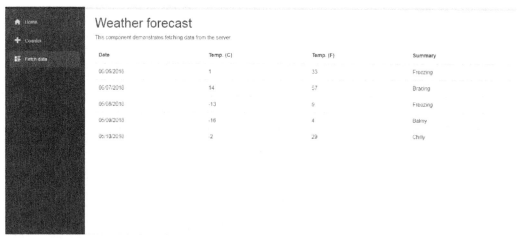

Figure 8.7: Blazor in action

20. In Solution Explorer, expand the Pages folder.

21. Open the **FetchData.razor** page to interrogate its code:

The code in **FetchData.razor** is used to display the weather forecast in an HTML page. It reads the weather information from a JSON file.

```
@page "/fetchdata"
@inject HttpClient Http

<h1>Weather forecast</h1>

<p>This component demonstrates fetching data from the server.</p>

@if (forecasts == null)
{
    <p><em>Loading...</em></p>
}
else
{
    <table class="table">
        <thead>
            <tr>
```

```
                <th>Date</th>
                <th>Temp. (C)</th>
                <th>Temp. (F)</th>
                <th>Summary</th>
            </tr>
        </thead>
        <tbody>
            @foreach (var forecast in forecasts)
            {
                <tr>
                    <td>@forecast.Date.ToShortDateString()</td>
                    <td>@forecast.TemperatureC</td>
                    <td>@forecast.TemperatureF</td>
                    <td>@forecast.Summary</td>
                </tr>
            }
        </tbody>
    </table>
}

@functions {
    WeatherForecast[] forecasts;

    protected override async Task OnInitAsync()
    {
        forecasts = await Http.GetJsonAsync<WeatherForecast[]>("s
ample-data/weather.json");
    }

    class WeatherForecast
    {
        public DateTime Date { get; set; }

        public int TemperatureC { get; set; }

        public int TemperatureF { get; set; }

        public string Summary { get; set; }
    }
}
```

Web API

ASP.NET Web **Application Programming Interface (API)** is a framework for building HTTP services that browsers, mobiles, and tablets can consume. It contains the ASP.NET MVC features such as routing, controllers, model binders and dependency injection.

ASP.NET Web API is the perfect platform for building RESTful applications using the .NET Framework. A RESTful application is an API that uses HTTP requests to GET, PUT, POST and DELETE data.

Web API supports the following features:

- Convention-based CRUD actions.

- Responses have Accept headers and HTTP status codes.

- Supports text formats such as XML and JSON.

- Supports OData automatically.

- Supports Self-hosting and IIS Hosting.

- Supports ASP.NET MVC features like routing and controllers.

Creating a new Web API application

Follow the next few steps to create a new Web API application:

1. Launch Visual Studio 2022.

2. Create a new ASP.NET Web Application.

3. Click **Create**.

4. Select Web API from the list shown as follows:

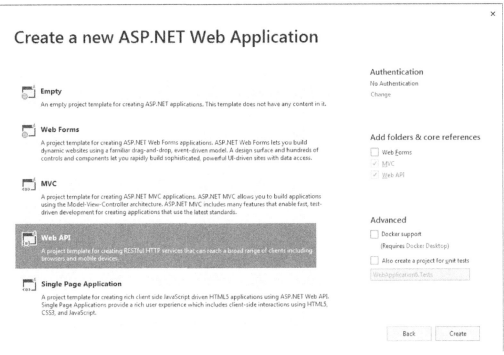

Figure 8.8: *Web API*

5. Click **Create**.

6. The created Views Controller looks like the following:

```
using System.Collections.Generic;
using System.Web.Http;

namespace WebApplication5.Controllers
{
    public class ValuesController : ApiController
    {
        // GET api/values
        public IEnumerable<string> Get()
        {
            return new string[] { "value1", "value2" };
        }

        // GET api/values/5
        public string Get(int id)
        {
```

```
        return "value";
    }

    // POST api/values
    public void Post([FromBody]string value)
    {
    }

    // PUT api/values/5
    public void Put(int id, [FromBody]string value)
    {
    }

    // DELETE api/values/5
    public void Delete(int id)
    {
    }
  }
}
```

7. The created **WebApiConfig** file looks like the following:

```
using System.Web.Http;

namespace WebApplication5
{
    public static class WebApiConfig
    {
        public static void Register(HttpConfiguration config)
        {
            // Web API configuration and services

            // Web API routes
            config.MapHttpAttributeRoutes();

            config.Routes.MapHttpRoute(
                name: "DefaultApi",
                routeTemplate: "api/{controller}/{id}",
```

```
                defaults: new { id = RouteParameter.Optional }
            );
        }
    }
}
```

Azure

Microsoft Azure is a cloud computing service designed for building, testing, deploying, and managing services and applications through managed data centres. Azure provides **Platform as a Service (PaaS)**, **Software as a Service (SaaS)**, and **Infrastructure as a Service (IaaS)**. It supports various different programming languages, tools, and frameworks, both Microsoft-specific and third-party software. We will explore Microsoft Azure throughout this book.

Conclusion

This chapter explored ASP.NET and web tools. We learned how important it is to have several tools working together. We looked at Web API and web frameworks. We especially had a look into the MVC web Framework which is the preferred framework to follow when developing websites. We also had a look at Cloud tools such as Kubernetes and Amazon Cognito.

The next chapter explores mobile tools in .NET. It covers what they are, where to find them and how to use them.

Key topics

- Blazor

- Azure

- .NET Core 3.1

Points to remember

- A web framework (or web application framework) is a framework that supports the development of web applications, web services, web resources, and web APIs.

- ASP.NET MVC is a web application framework that implements the MVC pattern.

- DNN Platform is a free, open source content management system.

- Blazor is a web framework that enables us to write client-side web applications using C# via WebAssembly and RAZOR.

Questions

1. Name three Web Frameworks.

2. What does Blazor enable us to do?

3. Name three Web API Features.

Answers

1. These include:

    a. ASP.NET MVC Framework

    b. DotNetNuke (DNN Platform)

    c. MonoRail

2. Blazor is a web framework that enables us to write client-side web applications using C# via WebAssembly and RAZOR.

3. These can include:

    a. Supports text formats such as XML and JSON.

    b. Supports OData automatically.

    c. Supports Self-hosting and IIS Hosting.

CHAPTER 9
Mobile Tools

Mobile devices have become part and parcel of what we are. Phones are not just phones anymore; they are mobile computers. We can send emails and use social media with the touch of a finger. We can edit and take photos and listen to and record music and videos.

We have become so dependent on our phones, tablets, and smartwatches that we cannot imagine a life without them anymore. Perhaps it is because the world has become so busy that we always need to be connected, or maybe it is because we are always connected that the world has become so busy. Mobile plays an essential role in the development scope. Integral.

Since we use mobile devices to stay connected, we, as programmers, must use the best tools at our disposal to create the best mobile experiences for users. Users are the keyword here. We develop everything for the users, and when they are not happy, the app will fail. As simple as that.

We must also remember that a company's website must look, feel and act the same way on a normal computer or laptop. Mobiles aren't just about apps.

Structure

In this chapter, we will cover the following topics:

- JSON

- Xamarin

- .NET MAUI

- Emulators and simulators

Objectives

In this chapter we will learn about mobile tools that can be used with Visual Studio 2022. We will learn about Xamarin and .NET MAUI to create a nice experience for the user. We will also touch on JSON and NuGet again. JSON is the quickest and best way to deal with any data. Lastly, we will talk about Emulators and Simulators.

JSON

JavaScript Object Notation (JSON) is a lightweight format for storing and transporting data from a server to a web page. JSON is quite easy to understand as it is self-describing.

JSON understands the following data types:

- **Number**: Any signed (positive or negative) decimal number that can contain fractions and exponential E notation. This number may not contain non-numbers such as NaN.

- **String**: Any sequence of zero or more Unicode characters.

- **Boolean**: Either true or false.

- **Array**: An ordered list of zero or more values.

- **Object**: (also called a key) an unordered collection of name–value pairs.

- **null**: An empty value.

JSON structure

Objects inside a JSON document are enclosed between curly braces and make use of commas to separate the name and value pairs. The name is on the left side and the value is on the right side. In-between is a colon. Arrays are enclosed with square brackets ([]) and make use of commas to separate each pair in the array.

Code listing shows an example JSON document.

```json
{
  "FirstName": "Ockert",
  "LastName": "du Preez",
  "Age": 40,
  "Address": {
    "StreetAddress": "135 Danie Smal Street",
    "City": "Meyerton",
    "Province": "Gauteng",
    "Country": "South Africa"
    "PostalCode": "1960"
  },
  "PhoneNumbers": [
    {
      "Type": "Office",
      "Number": "012 345 6789"
    },
    {
      "Type": "Mobile",
      "Number": "987 654 329"
    }
  ]
}
```

Without much trouble a person is able to figure out what information has been sent, in the example above. Personal details such as **FirstName**, **LastName** and **Age** is supplied. The **Address** is also provided, but it is also broken up into sub-pieces (**StreetAddress**, **City**, **Province**, **Country** and **PostalCode**). **PhoneNumbers** is an array which holds two entities – one entity for the office number, and another for the mobile number.

It gets more complicated, and the next topic will cover it.

JSON Schemas

A JSON Schema specifies a JSON-based format that defines the structure of JSON data for documentation, validation, and interaction control. A JSON Schema provides a contract for JSON data that is required by a given application, and how this data can then be modified.

A JSON document being validated is called **the instance**, the document that contains the description is called **the schema**.

An example JSON Schema looks like the following:

```json
{
  "$schema": "http://json-schema.org/schema#",
  "title": "Student",
  "type": "object",
  "required": ["StudentID", "StudentName", "StudentMarks"],
  "properties": {
    "StudentID": {
      "type": "number",
      "description": "Student Identifier"
    },
    "StudentName": {
      "type": "string",
      "description": "Name of Student"
    },
    "StudentMarks": {
      "type": "number",
      "minimum": 0
    },
    "StudentSubjects": {
      "type": "array",
      "items": {
        "type": "string"
      }
    },
  }
}
```

The JSON Schema above indicates that the **StudentID**, **StudentName** and **StudentMarks** fields are required. **StudentSubjects** is not required, although it is specified later in the schema. The properties for each fields are listed. These properties include the type of field as well as the description of the field. Lastly, the **StudentSubjects** field is supplied with its properties. It accepts an array of items of type string.

Now, we can use the above schema to test the validity of the following JSON code:

```
{
  « StudentID » : 1,
  « StudentName » : « Ockert »,
  « StudentMarks » : 99,
  « StudentSubjects » : [
    « C# »,
    « SQL »
  ]
}
```

This JSON data gets passed through the JSON Schema, and if it passes the validation, the data gets accepted and can be used.

Combining multiple subschemas

JSON Schema includes keywords for combining subschemas. Combining subschemas allows a certain array value to be validated against multiple criteria at the same time.

The keywords to combine schemas are:

- allOf
- anyOf
- oneOf
- not

Let's get into details of the above mentioned schema-combining-keywords.

allOf

The **allOf** keyword validates the JSON data against all of the subschemas. Keep in mind though, that when making use of the **allOf** keyword, it can be quite easy to create a logical impossibility. This means that two conflicting subschemas are created, thus causing the JSON data to always fail.

The next code segment illustrates how to make use of the **allOf** keyword to create a combined schema:

```
{
  "allOf": [
    { "type": "string" },
    { "maxLength": 9 }
  ]
}
```

This forces the supplied JSON array item to conform to its properties. The data must be a string and the maximum length of the supplied data is 9 characters. Any string longer than 9 characters will not be valid.

anyOf

The anyOf keyword ensures that the supplied JSON array item is valid against any (at least one) of the subschemas.

Here is an example of using **anyOf**:

```
{
  "anyOf": [
    { "type": "number" },
    { "type": "string" }
  ]
}
```

The above code sample accepts either a number or a string.

oneOf

When validating a JSON array item against **oneOf**, the supplied data must be valid against exactly one of the subschemas.

Here are two examples (which tests for the same data).

Example 1

```
{
  "oneOf": [
    { "type": "number", "multipleOf": 7 },
    { "type": "number", "multipleOf": 9 }
  ]
}
```

The supplied JSON data must either be a number which is a multiple of 7, for example 49, or 14; or a number that is a multiple of 9 such as 90, or 27.

Example 2 is a shortened version of Example 1 above.

Example 2

```
{
    "type": "number",
    "oneOf": [
      { "multipleOf": 7 },
      { "multipleOf": 9 }
    ]
}
```

not

The not keyword ensures that a given value validates when it doesn't validate against the supplied subschema.

An example follows:

```
{
    "not": {
        "type": "string"
    }
}
```

Any value supplied that isn't of type string, will be accepted. Any string value that is supplied, will not be valid.

Complex schemas

We can structure a JSON schema so that parts of it can be reused, instead of having to type the subschemas repeatedly. This is similar to writing a sub-procedure or method in C# that can be reused numerous times in a program. A simple example would be clicking the **Copy** button on a toolbar, or pressing *Ctrl* + *C*, or selecting **Edit**, **Copy**. Instead of writing the code three times, it can be written once and reused.

A Complex Schema can function the same way. Here is an example of having to write repetitive subschemas in a JSON Schema specification:

```
"HomeAddress": {
    "type": "object",
    "properties": {
```

```
    "StreetAddress": { "type": "string" },
    "City":             { "type": "string" },
    "Province":             { "type": "string" },
    "Country":             { "type": "string" }
  },
  "required": ["StreetAddress", "City", "Country"]
},
"WorkAddress": {
  "type": "object",
  "properties": {
    "StreetAddress": { "type": "string" },
    "City":             { "type": "string" },
    "Province":             { "type": "string" },
    "Country":             { "type": "string" }
  },
  "required": ["StreetAddress", "City", "Country"]
}
```

In the above code segment, **HomeAddress** and **WorkAddress** have the exact same properties, and expect the exact same data. This code can be shortened so that we can specify a section to be reused.

Let's have a look at the next example code segment.

```
{
  "definitions": {
    "Address": {
      "type": "object",
      "properties": {
        "StreetAddress": { "type": "string" },
        "City":             { "type": "string" },
        "Province":             { "type": "string" }
        "Country":             { "type": "string" }
      },
      "required": ["StreetAddress", "City", "Country"]
    }
  }
}
```

It is customary to create a key in your JSON Schema named "**definitions**" for reusable keys and properties. Now, to be able to reuse the **Address** key we need to make use of the **$ref** keyword.

The following code shows the use of the **$ref** keyword:

```
{ "$ref": "#/definitions/Address" }
```

To improve our previous code segment, we can now simply do this:

```
{
  "definitions": {
    "Address": {
      "type": "object",
      "properties": {
        "StreetAddress": { "type": "string" },
        "City":          { "type": "string" },
        "Province":        { "type": "string" },
        "Country":         { "type": "string" }
      },
      "required": ["StreetAddress", "City", "Country"]
    }
  },

  "type": "object",
  "properties": {
    "HomeAddress": { "$ref": "#/definitions/Address" },
    "WorkAddress": { "$ref": "#/definitions/Address" }
  }
}
```

Because **Address** is specified, we can reference it as many times as we need by using the **$ref** keyword, as the above code segment shows.

Xamarin

Xamarin apps contain native user interface controls which behave and looks familiar to the end-users. These apps have access to all the device's exposed functionality and can leverage platform-specific hardware acceleration.

Xamarin is currently (at the time of writing this book) the only IDE that enables native Android, iOS and Windows app development within Visual Studio 2022.

Xamarin provides add-ins to Visual Studio 2022 that enables developers to build apps easily within the Visual Studio IDE by using code completion and IntelliSense. Xamarin also has extensions within Visual Studio that supports building, deploying, and debugging of Xamarin apps on a simulator or directly on a device.

Installing Xamarin

To install Xamarin, follow these steps:

1. Download any of the Visual Studio 2022 suites from the Visual Studio page.

2. Start the installation.

3. Select the Mobile development with .NET workload from the installation screen, as shown next:

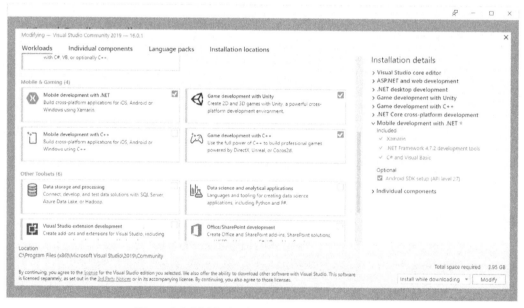

Figure 9.1: Mobile development with .NET Workload

4. Click the **Install** button in the lower right-hand corner.

Xamarin.Forms

Xamarin.Forms, a subset of Xamarin, is a cross-platform User Interface toolkit. This allows developers to create native user interface layouts that can be shared across platforms (Android, iOS, UWP). Xamarin.Forms allows you to share the business logic and data structures, and define the UI using common platform-independent controls.

Creating a Xamarin.Forms App

Use the next few steps to create a Xamarin.Forms application:

1. Click **File**.

2. Click **New**.

3. Click **Project**.

4. Choose **Mobile** from the Project type menu.

5. Select **Mobile App (Xamarin.Forms)** as shown next:

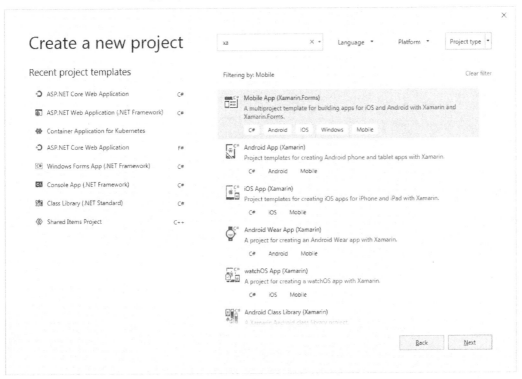

Figure 9.2: New Xamarin Project

6. Click **Next**.

7. Enter the project details.

8. Click **Create**.

9. Click on the Blank project type, as below.

10. Make sure Android and iOS are selected, as shown next:

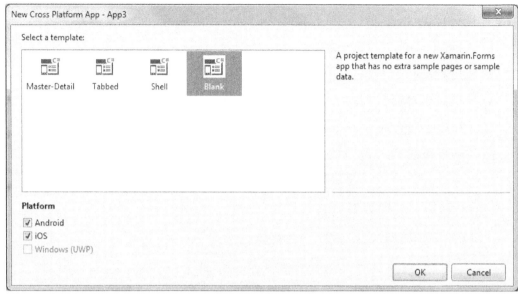

Figure 9.3: Blank Xamarin.Forms app

11. If necessary, accept the **Android Sdk licence**.

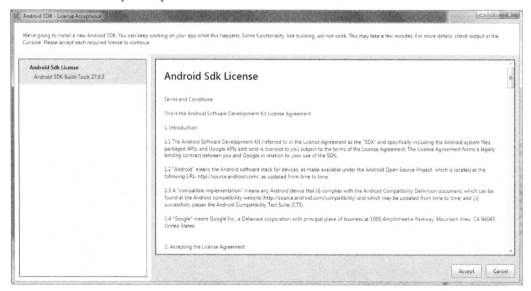

Figure 9.4: Android SDK License

12. After the project has loaded, open the **MainPage.xaml** file, and edit to look like the next code segment:

```xml
<?xml version="1.0" encoding="utf-8" ?>
<ContentPage xmlns="http://xamarin.com/schemas/2014/forms"
             xmlns:x="http://schemas.microsoft.com/winfx/2009/xaml"
             xmlns:local="clr-namespace:App3"
             x:Class="App3.MainPage">

    <StackLayout>
        <!-- Place new controls here -->
        <Label Text="Welcome to Xamarin.Forms!"
            HorizontalOptions="Center"
            VerticalOptions="CenterAndExpand" />

        <Button Text="Hello" Clicked="Button1_Clicked" />
    </StackLayout>

</ContentPage>
```

Edit **MainPage.xaml.cs** to look like the following code segment:

```csharp
using System.ComponentModel;
using Xamarin.Forms;

namespace App3
{
    // Learn more about making custom code visible in the
Xamarin.Forms previewer
    // by visiting https://aka.ms/xamarinforms-previewer
    [DesignTimeVisible(true)]
    public partial class MainPage : ContentPage
    {
        public MainPage()
        {
            InitializeComponent();
        }
        void Button1_Clicked(object sender, System.EventArgs e)
        {
            ((Button)sender).Text = $"Hello World!";
```

```
        }
      }
    }
```

13. Click on the Android Emulator button to start it. The **New Device Setup** dialog box may appear.

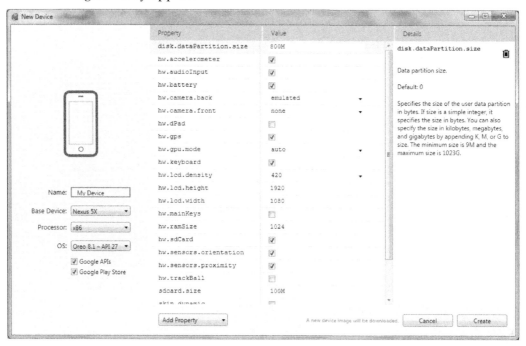

Figure 9.5: *New Device Setup*

14. The device will setup and be created. It might take a bit of time.

15. When the Emulator runs, it will display the little project that we have created. It will show the button with the initial caption of "Hello", and after it has been clicked, it will show "**Hello World!**" as shown below:

Figure 9.6: Our Xamarin app in action

.NET MAUI

.NET MAUI stands for .NET Multi-platform App UI. Simply put .NET MAUI is Xamarin.Forms that supports desktop apps. It provides a single stack that supports all modern workloads such as Android, iOS, macOS, and Windows. Each of these platform's native features are included in a cross-platform API with which you can deliver good user experiences while sharing code.

.NET MAUI enables us to use a single project that can target multiple platforms which allows us to quickly deploy to targets such as desktops, emulators, simulators, or physical devices with a single click.

With built-in cross-platform resources we can add any images, fonts, or translation files into a single project, and .NET MAUI automatically set up all the necessary native hooks, so we just have to code. With .NET MAUI we will always have access to the native operating system APIs. because everything is in one place, allowing developers to be more productive.

With .NET MAUI we will always have access to the native operating system APIs. because everything is in one place, allowing developers to be more productive.

It supports **Model-View-Update (MVU)** which provides a unified way to build cross-platform native front ends from a single code base, Blazor (an adaptive programming model for building web applications) development patterns, **Model-View-ViewModel (MVVM)**, and **ReactiveUI (RxUI)** like Xamarin.Forms does.

Emulators and simulators

A simulator is a virtual environment that models or mimics real-world applications such as flying and driving. An emulator is a software that allows computer software to function and behave identical to the way a certain software that is being emulated would.

Let's talk about Simulators and Emulators in a mobile programming environment. When an app needs to be tested, it can either be tested through connecting the physical device, or deploy the app to a physical device. Now, if there isn't a device available, what else can be done?

Differences between simulators or emulators to test apps

There are quite a few differences between simulators and emulators when it comes to testing mobile apps. The next table explains them:

Simulators	Emulators
A simulator simulates the internal state of an object very close to the internal state of an object.	An emulator emulates or mimics the outer behaviour of an object.
Whenever a developer or testing team needs to test a mobile device's external behaviour, simulators are preferable.	Whenever a developer or testing team needs to test the mobile device's internal behaviour, Emulators are preferable.
Simulators are usually written in high level programming languages.	Emulators are usually written in machine-level assembly languages.
Difficult to use for debugging.	More suitable to use for debugging.

Table 9.1: Differences between Simulators and Emulators

Visual Studio 2022 Android Emulator

A default Emulator gets installed when the Android SDK is installed, as shown previously in the Xamarin exercise. *Figure 9.8* shows the screen that pops up whenever the emulator is started, by running the application. This is the Android Device Manager, which is shown next:

Figure 9.7: *Android Device Manager*

The Android Device Manager displays various properties of the selected device. It shows the Android version, the processor, available memory and its resolution. It is a nice little feature where the emulator can be stopped and run independently.

Setting up a new device

Setting up a new device is quite simple. When the **New** button is clicked, in the Android Device Manager, the New Device window will appear, as shown in *Figure 9.5*. Here the various properties for the device can be changed. Properties not normally available, can also be added by selecting a property from the **Add Property** drop down list, as shown next:

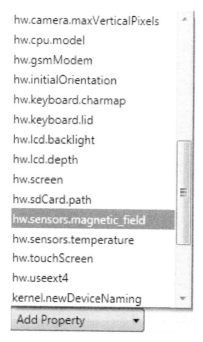

Figure 9.8: Add Property

Any of these properties can be added, and with the help of Xamarin, we get even more access to native device properties.

Conclusion

This chapter explored mobile tools. We explored JSON and JSON Schemas and learned how powerful it is to send information from and to the web server. We were introduced to Xamarin and DevExtreme, which can help us build native apps. Lastly, we learned how to test our mobile apps with Emulators and Simulators.

Chapter 10, Azure Tools explores Azure Tools in .NET. We will also explore Azure, Azure SDK, Docker and Azure IoT tools. It is a fun chapter!

Key topics

- Simulators
- Emulators

- .NET MAUI
- JSON

Points to remember

- JSON is a lightweight format for storing and transporting data from a server to a web page.

- A JSON Schema specifies a JSON-based format that defines the structure of JSON data for documentation, validation, and interaction control.

- Xamarin Apps contain native user interface controls which behaves and looks familiar to the end-users.

- .NET MAUI is Xamarin.Forms that supports desktop apps.

Questions

1. Describe the term JSON Schema.

2. What is the difference between a Simulator and an Emulator?

3. What is the difference between the allOf and anyOf JSON Schema keywords?

4. What tool do we use to install new Android devices to Emulate?

5. What is DevExtreme?

CHAPTER 10
Azure Tools

A zure is Microsoft's central Cloud computing platform. Without it, there simply wouldn't be Cloud Computing. There are cloud offerings from IBM, Google and Amazon, but Azure has always been one step ahead of its competitors. This chapter will introduce you to various Azure tools.

Structure

This chapter will cover the following Azure-based tools and technologies:

- Internet of Things
- SAP on Azure
- Artificial Intelligence
- DevOps
- Blockchain

Objectives

This chapter will cover all things related to Azure Cloud computing. After reading this chapter, you will have gained knowledge about Internet of Things, A. I. and Blockchain.

Azure

Microsoft Azure is a cloud computing service designed for building, testing, deploying, and managing services and applications through managed data centres. Azure provides **platform as a service (PaaS)**, **software as a service (SaaS)** and **infrastructure as a service (IaaS)**. It supports a variety of different programming languages, tools and frameworks, both Microsoft-specific and third-party softwares.

Azure provides numerous ready-to-go solutions including:

- Internet of Things
- SAP on Azure
- Artificial Intelligence
- DevOps
- Blockchain

Internet of Things

The **Internet of things (IoT)** is the expansion of Internet connectivity into physical devices and common everyday objects, such as kettles, TVs, fridges, and alarm systems - to name a few. Devices embedded with electronics, Internet connectivity, and sensors can communicate and interact with other devices over the Internet, and can be remotely monitored and controlled.

Azure for IoT reduces complexity, lowers costs and speeds up time to market. Azure for IoT is secure, open, and scalable. It includes the following:

- Azure IoT Hub
    - Azure IoT Hub is a managed service that is hosted in the cloud, which acts as a central message hub for bi-directional communication between the devices and the IoT application.
    - Azure IoT Hub is used to build IoT solutions with secure and reliable communications between IoT devices and a cloud-hosted solution backend. Azure IoT Hub supports numerous messaging patterns such as file upload from devices, device-to-cloud telemetry, and request-reply methods. Azure IoT Hub helps build scalable, full-featured IoT solutions.
- Azure IoT Edge
    - Azure IoT Edge moves custom business logic and cloud analytics to devices so that organizations can focus on business insights and not

data management. Analytics drives business value in IoT solutions. Azure IoT Edge contains three components:

- IoT Edge modules which are containers that run Azure services, third-party services, or custom code.

- The IoT Edge runtime that manages the modules deployed to each device.

- A cloud-based interface that enables remote monitoring and manages IoT Edge devices.

- Azure IoT Central

  o Azure IoT Central is a fully managed SaaS solution to connect, monitor and manage IoT assets at scale. It simplifies the initial setup of IoT solutions and reduces operational costs, the management and overhead of an IoT project.

- Azure IoT solution Accelerators

  o Azure IoT solution accelerators are complete, ready-to-deploy IoT solutions that implement common IoT scenarios. These include predictive maintenance, connected factory, remote monitoring, and device simulation. When deploying an Azure IoT solution accelerator, it includes all the required cloud-based services and any required application code.

- Azure Sphere

  o Azure Sphere is a solution for creating secured, connected **Microcontroller (MCU)** devices. Azure Sphere includes an operating system and an application platform which allows product manufacturers to create internet-connected devices that can be monitored, controlled, maintained and updated remotely.

- Azure Digital Twins

  o Azure Digital Twins is an Azure IoT service that can create comprehensive models of the physical environment. Azure Digital Twins can create spatial intelligence graphs to model relationships and interactions between spaces, devices and people. With Azure Digital Twins we can query data from physical spaces rather than from many discordant sensors. Azure Digital Twins has the following advantages:

    - The spatial intelligence graph which is a virtual portrayal of the physical environment.

    - Digital twin object models which are predefined device protocols and data schemas.

- ▪ Multiple and nested tenants.
- ▪ Advanced compute capabilities.
- ▪ Built-in access control.
- ▪ Ecosystem.

- Azure Time Series Insights
  - o Azure Time Series Insights stores, visualizes, and queries large amounts of time series data generated by IoT devices.
  - o Time Series Insights has these functions:
    - ▪ It connects to event sources and parses JSON from messages and structures in clean rows and columns.
    - ▪ It manages the storage of data. It stores data in memory and SSDs for up to 400 days.
    - ▪ It provides visualization with the help of the Time Series Insights explorer.

- Azure Maps
  - o Azure Maps provides developers powerful geospatial capabilities. It is an Azure One API compliant set of REST APIs for Maps, Search, Routing, Traffic, Mobility, Time Zones, Geolocation, Geofencing, Map Data, and Spatial Operations.

SAP on Azure

SAP on Azure solutions helps optimise **enterprise resource planning (ERP)** apps in the cloud, by using security features, reliability, and the scalable infrastructure of Azure.

The SAP on Azure solutions includes:

- SAP HANA
  - o SAP HANA on Azure handles transactions and analytics in-memory on a single data copy to accelerate business processes and gain business intelligence.
  - o SAP HANA on Azure offers the following:
    - ▪ On-demand M-series virtual machines certified for SAP HANA with 4 TB scale.
    - ▪ Purpose-built SAP HANA instances with 20 TB scale on a single node.
    - ▪ Scale out SAP HANA capabilities up to 60 TB.

- A 99.99 percent **service-level agreement (SLA)** for large instances in a high-availability pair.

- SAP S/4HANA
  - SAP S/4HANA is designed specifically for in-memory computing.
  - SAP S/4HANA on Azure offers the following:
    - Seamless connectivity for users accessing SAP Fiori-based applications whilst using Azure ExpressRoute.
    - A 99.99 percent SLA for critical ERP instances.
    - Backup for SAP S/4HANA and SAP B/4 HANA, with a low recovery-time objective.
    - Certification of SAP S/4HANA running on SUSE Linux Enterprise and Red Hat Enterprise Linux servers.

- SAP BW/4HANA
  - SAP BW/4HANA/SAP BW on HANA on Azure collects and connects to any data in real time with next-generation data warehouses that are built on SAP HANA.
  - SAP BW/4HANA/SAP BW on HANA on Azure offers the following:
    - Optimization of SAP Business Warehouses and analytics environments.
    - SAP Business Warehouse configurations that cannot fail.
    - Flexible scaling.
    - Certification that SAP BW/4HANA is running on SUSE Linux Enterprise and Red Hat Enterprise Linux.

- SAP NetWeaver
  - SAP NetWeaver on Azure offers the following:
    - Agility for non-production environments.
    - Cost-effective storage options.
    - 99.9 percent availability for single Virtual Machines.
    - SAP NetWeaver runs on Windows, SUSE Linux Enterprise and Red Hat Enterprise Linux.

- SAP Business One
  - SAP Business One provides more agility with on-demand VM infrastructures from Azure and it lowers non-production system costs via automation capabilities in Azure.

- SAP Business One on Azure offers the following:
  - 99.9 percent availability for single VMs.
  - SAP Business One runs on Azure Virtual Machines.

- SAP Hybris
  - SAP Hybris on Azure offers the following:
    - Business continuity via Azure Backup and Azure Site Recovery.
    - 99.9 percent availability for single VMs.
    - SAP Hybris Commerce Platform 5.x and 6.x runs on Windows Server, SQL Server and Oracle databases.

- SAP Cloud Platform
  - SAP Cloud Platform on Azure offers the following:
    - Cloud Foundry for managing cloud environments.
    - Co-locate applications using SAP ERP data.
    - Fast application development by using Azure Event Hubs and Azure Storage.

Artificial Intelligence

Artificial intelligence (AI) is the intelligence demonstrated by machines, whereas humans and animals display natural intelligence. Artificial intelligence is also used to describe machines that mimic cognitive (the ability to acquire knowledge and understanding through thought, experience, and senses) functions that humans associate with other human minds.

Artificial intelligence can be grouped into three types of systems:

- Analytical AI
  - Analytical AI has cognitive intelligence characteristics, these include using learning based on past experience to make future decisions and generating cognitive representation of the world.

- Human-inspired AI
  - Human-inspired AI contains elements from cognitive and emotional intelligence such as understanding human emotions and considering them in their decision making.

- Humanized AI

    o Humanized AI is self-conscious and is self-aware and has characteristics of all types of competencies such as cognitive, emotional, and social intelligence.

Microsoft AI platform

The Microsoft AI platform contains a suite of tools, such as the Bot Framework, Cognitive Services and Azure Machine Learning that allow developers to infuse AI into applications and scenarios, thus enabling intelligent experiences for their users.

The Microsoft AI platform (powered by Azure) supplies a set of interoperable services, APIs, libraries, frameworks and tools for developers. These include:

- **Cognitive services:** The Cognitive Services API capabilities are organized into vision, speech, language, knowledge and search. The APIs leverages pre-trained computer vision algorithms to recognize things such as landmarks, celebrities, face attributes, emotion, gender, and written words. Language capabilities analyzes key phrases, recognize commands from users, perform translations as well as spell check.

- **Customized computer vision models:** CustomVision.AI enables us to bring our own data, and use it to train the computer vision models.

- **Custom Machine Learning and Deep Learning Models:** Azure Machine Learning enables data scientists to build and manage models at scale. Data stores such as SQL, DB, CosmosDB, SQL Data Warehouse and **Azure Data Lake (ADL)** give access to the data that informs Machine Learning and deep learning models.

Azure AI

Microsoft Azure is a set of cloud services to help organisations meet their business challenges. AI is the capability of machines to imitate human behaviour. With Azure AI, machines can comprehend speech, analyse images, make predictions using data and interact in natural ways.

Azure AI is divided into three categories:

- Knowledge mining
- Machine learning
- API apps and agents

Knowledge mining

Knowledge mining uses Cognitive Search to find enterprise data with the help of Azure Search and Form Recognizer. This data can be emails, text files, documents, PDFs, images, scanned forms, and so on.

Azure Search is a cloud search service with built-in AI capabilities that enriches all types of information to identify and explore relevant content. Form Recognizer applies machine learning to extract text, key / value pairs, and tables from documents.

Machine Learning

Azure enables us to build, train and deploy machine learning models using Azure Machine Learning, Azure Databricks and ONNX. Azure Machine Learning is a Python-based service with automated machine learning and edge deployment capabilities. Azure Databricks is an Apache Spark-based big-data service with Azure Machine Learning integration. ONNX is an open-source model format and runtime for machine learning enabling us to move between frameworks and hardware platforms.

API Apps and Agents

These include Cognitive and the Bot Services. Let's do a practical exercise utilising a Cognitive Services API to detect a face or faces.

Use the following steps to create a free Azure account and subscribe to the desired Cognitive Services APIs:

1. Navigate to the following URL: **https://azure.microsoft.com/en-gb/free/?WT.mc_id=A261C142F**

2. Click on the **Start for Free** button as shown next:

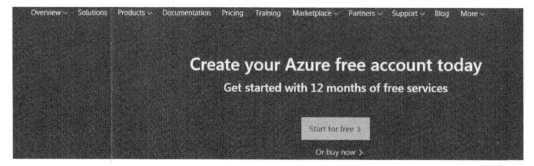

Figure 10.1: Start for Free

3. Follow the prompts and fill in the desired information.

4. Navigate to the next URL to subscript to the Face API: **https://azure.microsoft.com/try/cognitive-services/?api=face-api**

5. Click on the **Subscribe** button. This adds the subscription and supplies all the keys and EndPoints needed to create an app utilising the API, as shown next:

Your APIs   Hello ojdup

Face   Detect, identify, analyse, organise and tag faces in photos

This API key is currently active   30,000 transactions, 20 per minute.

7 days remaining   Endpoint: https://westcentralus.api.cognitive.microsoft.com/face/v1.0

                                          Key 1: 6e94db8d8df1405babec13d8f44627e7

                                          Key 2: 2586a797e8cc421aa9f49f7ff9f98116

Figure 10.2: *Keys*

Note: Keep in mind that each App gets its own unique set of keys

6. Launch Visual Studio 2019.

7. Create a new Console App (.NET Framework), as shown next:

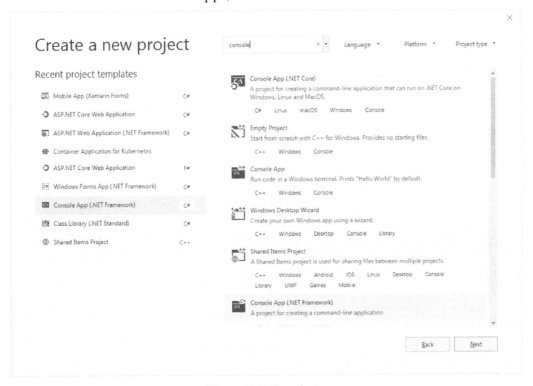

Figure 10.3: *Console App*

8. Click **Next**.

9. Supply a descriptive name and location for the project, and Click **Create**.

10. Add the necessary Namespaces at the top of the **Program.cs** file.

```
using System.IO;
using System.Net.Http;
using System.Net.Http.Headers;
```

11. Edit the **Program.cs** file to include the following code:

```
const string strKey = "YourKey"; //"6e94db8d8df1405bab-
ec13d8f44627e7";

const string strInputURL = "https://westcentralus.api.
cognitive.microsoft.com/face/v1.0";

static void Main(string[] args)
{
    string strPath = "http://www.OJ.com/OJ.jpg";

    if (File.Exists(strPath))
    {
        try
        {
            AnalyzeImage(strPath);
            Console.WriteLine("\nProcessing.\n");
        }
        catch (Exception e)
        {
            Console.WriteLine("\n" + e.Message);
        }
    }
}

static async void AnalyzeImage(string strURL)
{
    HttpClient hcClient = new HttpClient();

    hcClient.DefaultRequestHeaders.Add("Ocp-Apim-Sub-
```

```
scription-Key", strKey);

            string strParam = "returnFaceId=true&returnFaceLand-
marks=false" +

                "&returnFaceAttributes=age,gender,head-
Pose,smile,facialHair,glasses," +

                "emotion,hair,makeup,occlusion,accessories,blur,-
exposure,noise";

            string uri = strInputURL + "?" + strParam;

            HttpResponseMessage hrmResponse;

            byte[] btData = GetBytes(strURL);

            using (ByteArrayContent content = new ByteArrayCon-
tent(btData))
            {
                content.Headers.ContentType = new MediaTypeHead-
erValue("application/octet-stream");

                hrmResponse = await hcClient.PostAsync(uri, con-
tent);

                string strResponse = await hrmResponse.Content.
ReadAsStringAsync();

                Console.WriteLine(FormatOutput(strResponse));
            }
        }

        static byte[] GetBytes(string strURL)
        {
            using (FileStream fsFile = new FileStream(strURL,
FileMode.Open, FileAccess.Read))
            {
                BinaryReader brReader = new BinaryReader(fsFile);
                return brReader.ReadBytes((int)fsFile.Length);
            }
```

```
        }

        static string FormatOutput(string strJSON)
        {
            if (string.IsNullOrEmpty(strJSON))
                return string.Empty;

            strJSON = strJSON.Replace(Environment.NewLine, "").
Replace("\t", "");

            StringBuilder sbOutput = new StringBuilder();
            bool blnQuote = false;
            bool blnIgnore = false;
            int intOffset = 0;
            int intIndent = 4;

            foreach (char ch in strJSON)
            {
                switch (ch)
                {
                    case '"':
                        if (!blnIgnore) blnQuote = !blnQuote;
                        break;
                    case '\'':
                        if (blnQuote) blnIgnore = !blnIgnore;
                        break;
                }

                if (blnQuote)
                    sbOutput.Append(ch);
                else
                {
                    switch (ch)
                    {
                        case '{':
                        case '[':
                            sbOutput.Append(ch);
```

```
                            sbOutput.Append(Environment.NewLine);
                            sbOutput.Append(new string(' ', ++in-
tOffset * intIndent));

                            break;
                    case'}':
                    case ']':
                            sbOutput.Append(Environment.NewLine);
                            sbOutput.Append(new string(' ', --in-
tOffset * intIndent));

                            sbOutput.Append(ch);
                            break;
                    case ',':
                            sbOutput.Append(ch);
                            sbOutput.Append(Environment.NewLine);
                            sbOutput.Append(new string(' ', in-
tOffset * intIndent));

                            break;
                    case ':':
                            sbOutput.Append(ch);
                            sbOutput.Append(' ');
                            break;
                    default:
                            if (ch != ' ') sbOutput.Append(ch);
                            break;
                }
            }
        }

        return sbOutput.ToString().Trim();
    }
```

The code loads an image file from a supplied URL. It then analyses the image based on the parameters we gave. Finally, it provides an output in JSON format.

The resulting output from the above code may be similar to the following:

```
[
    {
        "faceId": "f6dde276-6421-44b4-8bdd-bc11c6dec812",
        "faceRectangle": {
            "top": 120,
            "left": 150,
            "width": 162,
            "height": 162
        },
        "faceAttributes": {
            "smile": 0.78,
            "headPose": {
                "pitch": 1.7,
                "roll": 2.3,
                "yaw": 3
            },
            "gender": "male",
            "age": 42.9,
            "facialHair": {
                "moustache": 0.7,
                "beard": 0.88,
                "sideburns": 0.06
            },
            "glasses": "sunglasses",
            "emotion": {
                "anger": 0.321,
                "contempt": 0.0,
                "disgust": 0.04,
                "fear": 0.02,
                "happiness": 0.495,
                "neutral": 0.023,
                "sadness": 0.0,
                "surprise": 0.005
```

```
    },
    "blur": {
        "blurLevel": "low",
        "value": 0.06
    },
    "exposure": {
        "exposureLevel": "goodExposure",
        "value": 0.78
    },
    "noise": {
        "noiseLevel": "low",
        "value": 0.15
    },
    "makeup": {
        "eyeMakeup": false,
        "lipMakeup": false
    },
    "accessories": [

    ],
    "occlusion": {
        "foreheadOccluded": false,
        "eyeOccluded": false,
        "mouthOccluded": false
    },
    "hair": {
        "bald": 0.67,
        "invisible": false,
        "hairColor": [
            {
                "color": "brown",
                "confidence": 0.04
            },
            {
```

```
                    "color": "black",
                    "confidence": 0.87
                },
                {
                    "color": "other",
                    "confidence": 0.51
                },
                {
                    "color": "blond",
                    "confidence": 0.08
                },
                {
                    "color": "red",
                    "confidence": 0.0
                },
                {
                    "color": "gray",
                    "confidence": 1.0
                }
            ]
        }
    }
}
]
```

Azure DevOps

Azure DevOps is a practice that unifies people, processes, technology, development and IT in five ways:

- Planning and tracking
- Development
- Build and test
- Delivery
- Monitoring and operations.

While practicing DevOps different teams from different disciplines such as development, IT operations, quality engineering and security, all work together.

Practising a DevOps model

Teams across different disciplines follow the following phases through their delivery pipeline.

- Plan and track
  - o Identify and track work visually by using practices such as Kanban boards and agile.

- Developing
  - o Write code with the help of version control systems such as Git to integrate continuously to the master branch.

- Build and test
  - o With an automated build process, the code is tested and validated immediately. This ensures that bugs are caught early in development.

- Deploying
  - o By using continuous delivery practices, the final deployment to production is ultimately a manually controlled business decision.

- Monitor and operate
  - o Once the app is live in production, monitoring delivers vital information about the app's performance and usage patterns.

Azure Blockchain Service

Blockchain is a transparent and verifiable system for exchanging values and assets. It is a shared, secure ledger of transactions distributed among a network of computers instead of a single provider. Azure Blockchain Service simplifies blockchain networks' formation, management and governance so developers can focus on business logic and app development.

Now that we know more about the Azure Blockchain Service, let's create a managed ledger by using the following steps:

1. Use the steps explained previously to create an Azure account, if necessary, else, sign in to the Azure portal by using this URL: **https://portal.azure. com/#home**

2. Select **Create a resource**.

3. Select **Blockchain | Azure Blockchain Service**, as shown next:

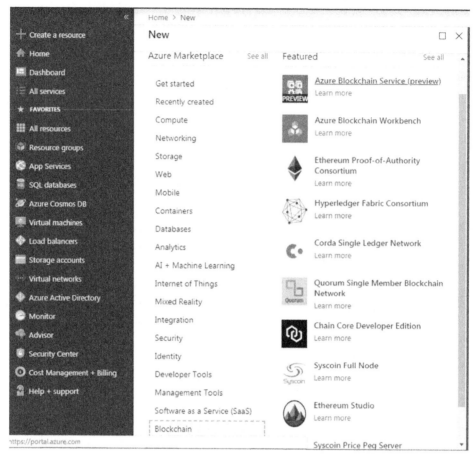

Figure 10.4: Blockchain Service

4. Select **Start Free**, if necessary.

5. Fill in the necessary details of the Blockchain member, as listed in the below table:

Property	Value
Blockchain Member	A unique name between 2 and 20 characters, containing only lowercase letters and numbers
Subscription	A valid Azure subscription
Resource Group	A resource group name (existing or new)
Region	Consortium members location
Member Account Password	Used to encrypt the private key for the Ethereum account created for the member.

Property	Value
Consortium name	A unique Consortium name
Description	Consortium Description
Protocol	Quorum protocol
Pricing	Node configuration for the new service
Transaction node password	Password for the new member's default transaction node

Table 10.1: Blockchain Member Properties

6. Select **Create**. The Blockchain member will be created.

Conclusion

This chapter explored Azure tools. We also explored Internet of Things in the Cloud, Blockchain and Artificial Intelligence.

In the next chapter we will explore the world of C++ 20.

Key topics

- Microsoft Azure
- Internet of things
- Artificial intelligence
- Azure DevOps
- Azure Blockchain Service

Points to remember

- Microsoft Azure is a cloud computing service designed for building, testing, deploying, managing services and applications through managed data centers.

- The IoT is the expansion of Internet connectivity into physical devices and common everyday objects, such as kettles, TVs, fridges, and alarm systems - to name a few.

- Blockchain is a transparent and verifiable system for exchanging values and assets.

Questions

1. Define the term Azure Blockchain Service.

2. Define the term Knowledge mining.

3. Define the term Microsoft AI Platform.

Answers

1. Azure Blockchain Service simplifies the formation, management and governance of blockchain networks so developers can focus on business logic and app development.

2. Knowledge mining is using Cognitive Search to find enterprise data with help of Azure Search and Form Recognizer.

3. The Microsoft AI platform contains a suite of tools, such as the Bot Framework, Cognitive Services and Azure Machine Learning that allow developers to infuse AI into applications and scenarios, thus enabling intelligent experiences for their users.

Section - IV
Advanced
Topics

Introduction

In the *Advanced Topics* section, we will discover all the new C++ 20 language features. We will create cross-platform applications with tools such as CMake, Look at Linux and WSL. Lastly, we will have a look at Visual Studio 2022 on Mac systems.

This section will have the following chapters:

- **Chapter 11**: C++ 20

- **APPENDIX A**:   Cross-Platform Applications

    Visual Studio for Mac

CHAPTER 11
C++ 20

With every new release of Visual Studio, comes a large amount of changes, especially in languages. C++ has been around for decades but keeps on evolving as a language.

Structure

In this chapter, we cover the following topic:

- New C++ 20 language features

Objectives

In this chapter we will have a look at the new language features in C++ 20.

New C++ 20 language features

A lot of C++ 20 features have been built into Visual Studio 2022.

Let's go into more detail.

Language features

Language features include the following:

- New attributes
- New specifiers
- Aggregate initialization
- Designated initializers
- Modules
- Abbreviated function templates

New attributes

C++ 20 provides the following new attributes:

- **no_unique_address**
- **likely**
- **unlikely**

Let's break them down:

- **no_unique_address**

  With the **no_unique_address** attribute data members can become overlapped with other non-static data members or base class subobjects. A short example follows:

  ```
  #include <iostream>

  struct Empty {};
  struct A {
      int aa;
      Empty ee;
  };
  struct B {
      int bb;
      [[no_unique_address]] Empty ee;
  };
   struct C {
      char cc;
  ```

```
    [[no_unique_address]] Empty e1, e2;
};
struct D {
    char dd[2];
    [[no_unique_address]] Empty e1, e2;
};

int main()
{
    static_assert(sizeof(Empty) >= 1);

    static_assert(sizeof(A) >= sizeof(int) + 1);
    std::cout << "sizeof(B) == sizeof(int) is " << std::boolalpha
            << (sizeof(B) == sizeof(int)) << '\n';
    static_assert(sizeof(C) >= 2);
    std::cout << "sizeof(D) == 2 is " << (sizeof(D) == 2) <<
'\n';
}
```

In the above code segment we first created an empty class, then four structs that references it with the **no_unique_address** attribute. In the main method we determine which of the objects can have the same address.

- **likely and unlikely**

  The likely and unlikely attributes gives the compiler an opportunity optimizer for the case where paths of execution (which includes either likely or unlikely) are more or less likely than any alternative path of execution. A small example follows.

```
int ex(int x)
{
    switch(x)
    {
        case 1: [[fallthrough]];
        [[likely]] case 2: return 1;
    }
    return 2;
}
```

In this case, x == 2 is more likely than any other value of x.

New specifiers

C++ 20 contains two new specifiers. They are:

- Consteval
- Constinit

Let's have a look at them individually.

Consteval

consteval makes a function an immediate function. As normal functions should return a value, every call to a function signified as consteval, must produce a compile-time constant. Some examples are as follows:

```
consteval int sqr(int number) {
  return number*number;
}
constexpr int result = sqr(200);
```

Another example:

```
constexpr int i = function();
```

Constinit

constinit ensures that a variable has static initialization - either zero initialization or constant initialization. For example:

```
constinit const char *c = func(true);
```

Aggregate initialization

As many experienced C++ developers would know, Aggregate Initialization simply initializes aggregates. Some examples of the braced initializers available in C++ 20 follows:

```
T object = { .designator = argument1 , .designator { argument2 } ... };
T object { .designator = argument1 , .designator { argument2 } ... };
T object (argument1, argument2, ...);
```

An aggregate can be any of the following types:

- No user-provided, inherited, or explicit constructors

- No user-declared or inherited constructors

Designated initializers

Designated initialization in C++ 20 is a form of aggregate initialization.

Instead of writing an aggregate initialization, we write a code like the following code segment which is similar to what we have seen in the aggregate initializations preceding code section:

```
Type obj = { .designator = value, .designator = value2, ... };
```

or

```
Type obj = { .designator { value }, .designator { value2 }, ... };
```

We can write.

```
struct Point {
    string name { "BpB" };
    string surname { "Publications" };
};
```

Coroutines

A coroutine in C++ 20 is a function that suspends execution which can be resumed at a later stage. Coroutines suspend execution by returning to the caller. The data that is then required to resume execution is stored separately from the stack making Coroutines stackless.

Coroutines make use of any of the following in their definitions :

- **co_await**
- **co_yield**
- **co_return**

Let's have a look at small examples of each.

Coroutines make use of any of the following in their definitions:

- **co_await**

  co_await suspends execution until it's rersumed. A small example follows:
  ```
  task<> tcp_echo_server() {
    char data[1024];
    while (true) {
      size_t n = co_await socket.async_read_some(buffer(data));
  ```

```
      co_await async_write(socket, buffer(data, n));
    }
}
```

For more information and examples (like the one above) on **co_await**, please refer to the *References* section at the end of this chapter.

- **co_yield**

  co_yield suspends execution and returns a value. A small example follows:

```
generator<int> iota(int n = 0) {
  while(true)
    co_yield n++;
}
```

For more information and examples (like the one above) on **co_yield**, please refer to the *References* section at the end of this chapter.

- **co_return**

  co_return completes execution and returns a value. A small example follows:

```
lazy<int> f() {
  co_return 7;
}
```

For more information and examples (like the one above) on co_return, please refer to the *References* section at the end of this chapter.

Modules

With modules we can share declarations and definitions across translation units.

A simple example follows:

```
// helloBpB.cpp
export module helloBpB;  // define module
import <iostream>;
export void hello() {      // method to be exported
    std::cout << "Hello BpB!\n";
}
// main.cpp
```

```
import helloBpB;  // import hellpBpB module


int main() {
    hello(); //make use of hello method in the helloBpB.cs translation
unit
}
```

Abbreviated function templates

When a parameter list or a function template declaration contains a placeholder type such as auto or Concept auto, the declaration declares a function template, and one invented template parameter for each placeholder is appended to the template parameter list. Some examples of the template parameter list follow:

```
void function1(auto); // same as template<class T> void function(T)
```

```
void function2(concept1 auto); // same as template<C1 T> void
function2(T), if concept1 is a concept
```

```
void function3(concept2 auto...); // same as template<C2... Ts> void
function3(Ts...), if concept2 is a concept
```

```
void function4(const concept3 auto*, concept4 auto&); // same as
template<concept3 T, concept4 U> void function4(const T*, U&);
```

Conclusion

In this chapter, the first chapter in the *Advanced Topics* section, we got a quick look at the new C++ 20 language features.

In the *APPENDIX* , we will cover *Cross-Platform Applications*, details creating cross-platform apps on different platforms with tools such as CMake, Linux, and WSL, and Visual Studio for Mac features.

Key topics

- C++ 20
- Coroutines
- Function templates
- Attributes

Points to remember

- With the `no_unique_address` attribute, data members can become overlapped with other non-static data members or base class subobjects.

- The `likely` and `unlikely` attributes give the compiler an opportunity to optimize for cases where paths of execution (which include either likely or unlikely) are more or less likely than any alternative path of execution.

Questions

1. Explain the term: Consteval

2. Explain the term: Aggregate Initialization

3. Explain the function of the `likely` and `unlikely` attributes.

Answers

1. consteval - Makes a function an immediate function.

2. Aggregate Initialization simply initializes aggregate.

3. The `likely` and `unlikely` attributes allow the compiler an opportunity to optimize for the cases where paths of execution (which include either likely or unlikely) are more or less likely than any alternative path of execution.

References

Coroutines: https://en.cppreference.com/w/cpp/language/coroutines

Appendix
'A'

Introduction

In this Appendix, we will quickly look at Cross-Platform applications and Visual Studio for Mac.

Structure

In this Appendix, we will cover the following topics:

- Cross-Platform Applications
  - CMake
  - WSL

- Visual Studio for Mac
  - Git
  - macOS accessibility features
  - Color Coded Tabs
  - Vertical tabs
  - Linux Support

Objectives

We will quickly have a look at some Cross-Platform abilities in Visual Studio 2022, including CMake options and WSL for Linux. After reading this Appendix, you will also understand what Visual Studio 2022 can do on Mac.

Cross-platform applications

Some cross-platform applications are mentioned below:

CMake

CMake is a cross-platform, open-source tool for defining build processes that run on multiple platforms.

Installing CMake on Visual Studio is quite easy:

Install the **C++ Linux workload** in the Visual Studio installer. This installs the C++ CMake tools as well. Both C++ CMake tools for Windows and Linux Development with C++ are required for cross-platform CMake development.

For more information on configuring, follow this link: **https://docs.microsoft.com/ en-us/cpp/build/cmake-projects-in-visual-studio?view=msvc-170**

WSL

Windows Subsystem for Linux

With Visual Studio 2022 (version 17.0 or higher) comes a new native C++ toolset for the Windows Subsystem for Linux version 2 (or WSL 2) development. The Windows Subsystem for Linux enables developers to run a GNU/Linux environment with its command-line tools, utilities, and applications on Windows.

Visual Studio 2022 allows developers to:

- Invoke Windows applications using a Unix-like command-line shell.

- Invoke GNU/Linux applications on Windows.

- Run Bash shell scripts and GNU/Linux command-line applications.

- Run vim (configurable text editor), emacs (family of text editors characterized by their extensibility), and tmux (open-source terminal multiplexer for Unix-like operating systems).

- Run command-line tools such as **Global regular expression print (grep)**, **Stream editor (sed)**, *Aho, Weinberger, Kernighan* (**awk**) – authors), or other **Executable and Linkable Format (ELF-64)** binaries.

More information on grep, sed, awk, and ELF-64 follows:

Grep

A grep filter searches a file for a given pattern of characters. This pattern is referred to as the regular expression.

Its basic syntax looks like the following:

```
a) grep [options] pattern [files]
```

Following is a breakdown of all the options for a grep regular expression:

Options	Description
b) -c	Prints the count of lines matching the pattern
c) -h	Displays matched lines.
d) -i	Ignores casing
e) -l	Displays list of file names
f) -n	Displays matched lines with their line numbers
g) -v	Prints all lines that do not match
h) -e exp	Specifies expressions
i) -f	Takes patterns from a file
j) -E	Treats pattern as an ERE (extended regular expression)
k) -w	Matches whole word
l) -o	Prints matching parts of a line
m) -A	Prints the line being searched after the result
n) -B	Prints the line being searched before the result
o) -C	Prints the line being searched before and after the result

Appendix Table 1: grep options

Sed

The **sed** command contains functions to search files, find and replace (most used) in files, insertion, or deletion into and from files. **sed** also supports regular expressions that can perform complex pattern matching. An example follows:

```
sed '/^ *$/d' inputFileName
```

This looks complicated, but it demonstrates the most acceptable regular expressions. These are as follows:

Regular Expression symbol	Description
^ (caret)	Matches the beginning of the line
$ (dollar sign)	Matches the end of the line
* (asterisk)	Matches zero or more occurrences of the previous character
+ (plus)	Matches one or more occurrence(s) of the previous character
? (question mark)	Matches zero or one occurrence of the previous character
. (dot)	Matches exactly one character

Appendix Table 2: sed regular expression options

Awk

Awk is a scripting language used to manipulate data and generate reports. Awk requires no compiling and allows the developer to use variables, numeric functions, string functions, and logical operators.

With Awk, developers can write small programs containing statements that define text patterns to be searched for in each document line, as Awk is mainly used for pattern scanning and processing. Awk can search files to see if they contain lines matching the specified patterns and perform the associated actions.

Installing WSL on Windows and Visual Studio 2022

To install the WSL command in Windows, follow these steps:

1. In PowerShell (Windows key, search for PowerShell, or type in PowerShell), enter the following command:

    ```
    wsl –install
    ```

    For more detailed information on installing WSL on Windows, have a look here: **https://docs.microsoft.com/en-us/cpp/build/walkthrough-build-debug-wsl2?view=msvc-170**

Installing the Build tools for Visual Studio 2022

2. Install WSL, as previously mentioned.

3. Use the following commands to install the required tools on WSL 2 distro:

    ```
    sudo apt update

    sudo apt install g++ gdb make ninja-build rsync zip
    ```

4. This installs a C++ compiler, CMake (as discussed earlier), rsync, and zip.

Visual Studio for Mac

Following are some good links to work with various aspects of Visual Studio for mac:

Git: https://docs.microsoft.com/en-us/visualstudio/mac/working-with-git?view=vsmac-2022

macOS accessibility features: https://docs.microsoft.com/sr-latn-rs/visualstudio/mac/accessibility?view=vsmac-2019

Color Coded Tabs: https://tabsstudio.com/documentation/color-coded-tabs-in-visual-studio.html

Linux Support: https://visualstudio.microsoft.com/vs/mac/

Conclusion

This concludes the book. We have learned a lot about how to work with Visual Studio 2022 in all aspects and areas of development. The Visual Studio 2022 IDE boasts a host of impressive tools that can do anything from helping with typing in code with IntelliCode to working with Azure and Mac.

It has been a long journey, and remember: a book is not meant to gather dust.

Index

Printed in Great Britain
by Amazon

47449994R00145